KAYAK TOURING & CAMPING

KAYAK TOURING & CAMPING

CECIL KUHNE

STACKPOLE
BOOKS

Published by
STACKPOLE BOOKS
5067 Ritter Road
Mechanicsburg, PA 17055
www.stackpolebooks.com

Printed in the United States

10 9 8 7 6 5 4 3 2 1

First edition

Library of Congress Cataloging-In-Publication Data
Kuhne, Cecil, 1952-
    Kayak touring and camping / Cecil Kuhne. —1st ed.
      p. cm.
    Includes bibliographical references (p.).
    ISBN 0-8117-2843-9
    1. Kayak touring. 2. Kayak touring Equipment and supplies.
3. Camping. 4. Camping Equipment and supplies. I. Title.
GV&89.K85 1999   98-46617
797.1'224—dc21   CIP

To Cherie, naturally

CONTENTS

ACKNOWLEDGMENTS

I owe a great deal to the skilled editors at Stackpole Books, particularly Mark Allison and Dave Richwine, for their editorial expertise and kindly encouragement.

My friends at Nantahala Outdoor Center were, as always, instrumental in keeping my enthusiasm for paddling at an all-time high. Likewise the editors at *Canoe & Kayak* magazine, where I am proud to serve as contributing editor.

And lastly, but most importantly, I am indebted to my wonderful wife, Cherie, for her good-natured tolerance for a writing and kayaking passion that sometimes gets a little out of hand.

INTRODUCTION

This is a book about the equipment and techniques of overnight touring by kayak—whether it be a quiet journey into a sheltered cove, an exploration of the shorelines of one of the Great Lakes, a peaceful afternoon on a neighborhood pond, a rigorous island crossing, or a meander down a lazy river.

Kayak touring has recently exploded in popularity around the country, and for anyone who has ever picked up a paddle and tried it, it's easy to understand why. First of all, the basic techniques necessary to get started are easy to master, and with a few hours of practice, you can become reasonably proficient at paddling in mild conditions. Second, the touring kayak can accommodate a fair amount of gear for overnight excursions, and with little effort you can take along some of the modern conveniences you never dreamed of when backpacking. Third, the number and diversity of destinations for pursuing the endeavor are truly infinite. What other outdoor pursuit can you say these things about?

Let's start off by clarifying a common misconception about the boats used for kayak touring. There are basically two types of "touring" boats—casual recreational boats and sea kayaks. A sea kayak is a touring boat, but a casual recreational boat is *not* a sea kayak. In other words, a casual recreational boat is somewhat limited in the journeys it is competent to handle. This is because such boats are usually made to be more stable (which is helpful to beginners), but with that stability comes a loss of maneuverability in heavy waves. A sea kayak, of course, can be used on family jaunts across the neighborhood pond, but it's a little overqualified for that particular journey. If you're interested in taking an extended or arduous voyage along the coastline, however, the sea kayak is the boat you'll need.

The beauty of kayak touring is the range of trips you can undertake. A lot of boaters never venture beyond the nearby lake or stream and therefore don't feel compelled to learn about fancy compasses or global positioning systems, or even how to Eskimo-roll the kayak in a capsize. In fact, most touring kayakers are not interested in open crossings of large bodies of water and the special equipment, techniques, and precautions that such expeditions entail. Most of us are quite content to spend a week cruising the Baja, paddling part of the Inside Passage from Seattle to Alaska, exploring

Lake Superior, touring the Maine coast, floating down the Rio Grande, cruising the San Juan Islands, and the thousand-and-one other adventures that are possible for an ordinary mortal in a touring kayak.

It is for these boaters that this book is written, and I wish you the same joys I have experienced in this most mystical of endeavors. Welcome aboard, fellow paddlers, and *bon chance!*

GREAT RIVER OUTFITTERS

The number and diversity of kayak touring destinations are truly infinite.

PART I

EQUIPMENT

1

THE TOURING KAYAK

The touring kayak is an inspired design—simple, efficient, and highly adaptable. Its sleek form glides effortlessly through the water, yet it is quite capable of handling the roughest wind and waves. Properly packed, it can carry enough gear for weeks at a time. It is, in short, a creation perfectly suited to its place and purpose.

Though simple in concept, touring kayaks are available in an amazingly wide array of designs. We'll look at both recreational touring kayaks, designed for casual forays into gentle rivers, lakes, and other sheltered waters, and sea kayaks, designed for more rugged use in the ocean. But first, a little terminology may be in order for those new to the sport. The *bow* is the front of the boat, and the *stern* the rear. The *hull* is the bottom half of the boat, and the top half is the *deck*. The point where the two meet is called the *gunwale* (pronounced "gunnel"). The hull and deck can be made from a variety of materials such as fiberglass or wood, though most are now made of molded polyethylene. Naturally, the kayak has a *seat* of some kind, and for added control and comfort, it has *foot braces* as well.

The *cockpit* is the opening where you sit, and it has a lip, called a *coaming*, over which the *spray skirt* fits to keep out water. To add structural rigidity and flotation, most boats have internal *bulkheads* of some sort behind the cockpit and in front of the foot braces, and *hatches* of some kind to allow access into those compartments for storing personal gear. Many touring boats have a *rudder* or a *skeg* to aid in directional control of the boat.

At the ends of the kayak are short lengths of rope (often with plastic togglelike handles attached) called *grab loops*. Many touring boats have elastic cords called *deck bungees* attached to the top of the boat for holding maps, bilge pumps, spare paddles, and other items that need to be handy.

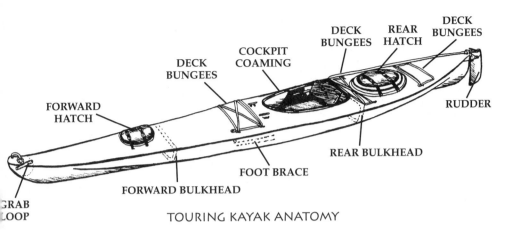

DECK
BUNGEES

COCKPIT
COAMING

DECK
BUNGEES

DECK
BUNGEES

REAR
HATCH

DECK
BUNGEES

FORWARD
HATCH

RUDDER

GRAB
LOOP

REAR BULKHEAD

FOOT BRACE

FORWARD BULKHEAD

TOURING KAYAK ANATOMY

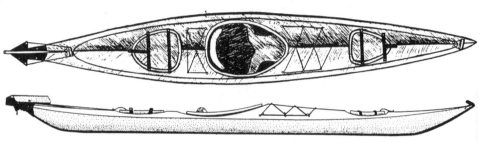

TOURING KAYAK: TOP AND SIDE VIEWS

It's important to note that every touring design is a compromise of sorts. There is no such thing as the ideal touring kayak—only the ideal touring kayak for your particular needs. You must identify those needs—by deciding what type of touring you'll be doing most of the time—before you make the final decision about which boat to buy.

CHOOSING A TOURING KAYAK

Kayaks designed for backcountry travel are asked to do just about everything—carry big loads, endure heavy waves, maintain directional stability, and be relatively easy and fast to paddle. Entry lines must be slim enough to ease paddling, but then flare somewhat to improve buoyancy and carrying capacity.

Kayaks have changed dramatically in recent years. Gone are the days of all-purpose kayaks. Manufacturers are now producing a variety of specialized boats in an amazing combination of designs. The first step is to study the myriad choices, keeping in mind that all kayaks are a compromise between speed, maneuverability, and stability.

Speed. A long, thin design inevitably travels faster than a short, wide one. Having more of a V-shaped bottom that extends the length of the boat helps it run straighter. Then all your energy can be directed toward making the boat go fast.

Maneuverability. A short, wide boat is generally more maneuverable than a long, skinny one. As a result, a fast and maneuverable boat is something of a contradiction.

Stability. A wide design is usually more stable than a narrow one. Also, a flat-bottomed boat, or one with a shallow V-shaped bottom, at first seems more stable than one with a rounded U-shaped hull. So if you want initial stability, you can't have speed.

TOURING KAYAK DESIGN

Kayakers, if anything, are an opinionated lot. They know what they like to paddle, and they'll be glad to tell you about it. A long evening engaged in such conversation will no doubt yield a variety of viewpoints on seemingly esoteric topics of design. But the general principles of kayak design are really quite simple.

Hull shape. Hulls with flat bottoms, hard chines (sharp, nearly right-angle edges where bottom and sides meet), and greater flare (curvature of the sides outward) have greater stability. Conversely, round hulls with soft chines (a gradual curve where bottom and sides meet) and less flare on the sides have much less stability but are more nimble and easier to roll if they should tip over.

Bow shape. A long, skinny kayak with a bow shaped like a narrow V is fast because the bow slices through the water rather than bashing into it and piling it up in front of the boat. A kayak that is broad in the beam and carries that fullness forward and aft is a freighter, not a racer. That kayak may be great for carrying big loads and riding waves, but it will not be quick. Most kayaks fall somewhere in between.

Single versus tandem boats. Most kayaks are made for a single paddler, but tandem, or double, kayaks, where one paddler sits directly behind the other, are also made for touring. In most of these double models, separate cockpits are provided; in some, there is one large, open cockpit.

Sit-on-tops. A relatively new concept, the sit-on-top kayak appeals to those who feel claustrophobic in an enclosed cockpit. Although these boats are increasing in popularity, the number of models available is limited. Because of design and space considerations, most of these models are suitable only for short, leisurely forays.

A knowledgeable kayak dealer can be helpful in making decisions about design. Better yet is an association with a kayak club where you can meet others who have paddled various models and who will let you try your hand at paddling their boats. There's nothing, after all, like on-the-water testing to determine how you like a particular model. At the very least, you should rent before you buy—it's too big an investment to do otherwise.

Tandem, or double, kayaks are popular for touring.

LENGTH

The length of a kayak has a tremendous effect on its tracking, maneuverability, and stability. The range generally varies from casual recreation models that are 12 or 13 feet long to double-seated expedition boats that are 20 or more feet in length.

Longer kayaks have a number of advantages: They are usually easier to paddle, more stable with the same amount of weight, and capable of carrying heavier loads with less loss of performance. They also track better, move faster, and glide farther with each stroke, allowing greater efficiency with less effort. These attributes are especially important on lakes or other calm water, where hairpin turns are not involved.

With a shorter kayak, you (oddly enough) have to exert more energy to paddle it forward than with a longer model. A longer kayak also negotiates wind-tossed waves more smoothly than a short one. A shorter boat torques out with each oncoming wave, which leaves you fighting to keep on course. Add more length, and you suddenly gain stability and a much better ride. Increase the length even more, and the craft becomes completely manageable, rising and falling gently with the waves.

Shorter kayaks are lighter, less expensive, less cumbersome, and easier to transport. But the most important virtue of a short kayak is quicker turns. A short hull is also preferable for paddling on narrow streams and for small people or children.

WIDTH

The width of a kayak has a definite influence on the boat's handling characteristics. The primary function of width is stability. Wider boats are usually more stable and are often recommended for beginners. But handling is sacrificed for that extra width, and the kayak does not work as well in current. A narrower boat increases the boat's efficiency because it brings the paddler's forward strokes closer to the centerline of the kayak.

Additional width adds to carrying capacity (though not as much as length does), but kayaks that are too wide require greater effort to paddle, simply because their hulls push more water.

CHINES

The transition between the bottom of the kayak and its sides is called the chine. An abrupt, nearly right-angle transition is called a hard chine, and a smoother, more rounded one is a soft chine. Hard chines have great initial stability but almost no secondary stability. Soft chines have less initial stability but better secondary stability.

HARD CHINE   SOFT CHINE

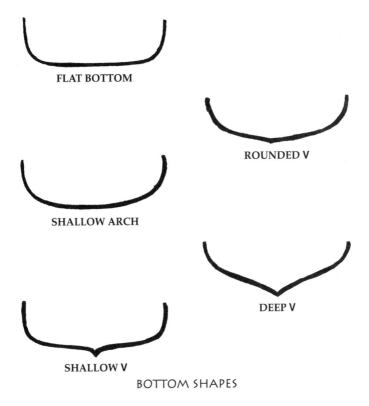

FLAT BOTTOM

ROUNDED V

SHALLOW ARCH

DEEP V

SHALLOW V

BOTTOM SHAPES

BOTTOM SHAPES

The bottom of a kayak (as viewed from its end) ranges from flat-bottomed to V-shaped. Flat-bottomed kayaks seem very stable when you first get into the boat and it is level. More rounded hulls are initially less stable than flat bottoms, but they have greater secondary stability when the boat is leaned on its edge and are better able to handle waves. The more pronounced the V shape on the bottom, the better the boat's directional control, but the worse its stability.

FLARE

The angle of a kayak's sides outward is called the flare. Kayaks with flared sides have greater secondary stability, and though they are less stable initially, they are easier to edge or lean for turning. For casual touring in smooth water, the widest, least flared, most flat-bottomed boat is what you need.

SYMMETRY

A kayak's symmetry is the overall shape of the boat from front to back. Some boats are symmetrical, which means that the front half and the back half of the kayak have the same shape, and some are asymmetrical.

Symmetry affects not only the efficiency of the boat as it moves through water but also its ability to turn. Symmetrical boats are better for quick maneuvering, as in negotiating small streams. Asymmetrical boats usually lengthen and streamline the bow for more efficient and faster passage through the water. Directional control and speed are increased, but turning ability is decreased.

There are two types of asymmetrical shapes: fish-form and Swede-form. Fish-form has more volume fore (ahead) of the midpoint, and Swede-form has more volume aft of (behind) the midpoint. Both designs work well in touring boats.

TAPER

The taper, or entry lines, of a kayak's bow and stern (as viewed from above) is usually described as either full or pointed. A boat with full ends gives the bow extra volume for extra storage and for riding over a wave that would otherwise bury it. A fast cruiser has a very fine, thin bow to knife through the water more easily.

ROCKER

The upturn of the kayak from one end to the other (as viewed from the side of the kayak) is known as rocker. Many touring kayaks have little or no rocker. The flatter the line, the easier it is to keep the kayak on a straight course, but the more difficult it is to maneuver. With more lift at its ends, turning is easier.

Kayaks with rocker pivot more easily because the ends of the kayak sit higher in the water and offer less resistance, but these boats do not track well. Touring kayaks with little rocker move in a straight line more easily because the boat resists the turning forces of paddling strokes. These boats do not turn easily because the entire hulls sits in the water.

All kayaks are a composite design of sorts.

VOLUME

Volume is the amount of space occupied by the interior of the boat, which is sometimes expressed in terms of gallons. Volume naturally has an effect on the buoyancy of the boat and on the paddler's comfort and fit. It is especially important if you take long trips requiring the storage of gear.

WEIGHT

A kayak's weight is largely a function of its materials (discussed in detail later). Naturally, the lighter the boat, the easier it is to maneuver. But weight is often sacrificed at the expense of durability.

KAYAK INTERIORS

Any kayak can be customized to suit your individual needs (see the section "Customizing Your Kayak"). Most kayaks arrive from the factory in fairly spartan condition but usually contain the following:

Seats. The type and placement of seats vary, affecting not only comfort but also the handling of the boat. A lower seat, for example, provides greater stability because it lowers the center of gravity. The seat should be snug to provide better control, and additional closed-cell foam can be added for this purpose.

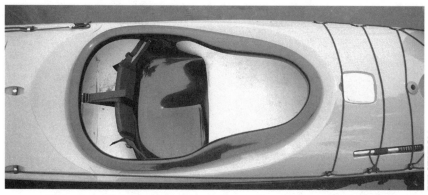

PERCEPTION

The type and placement of seats affect both comfort and handling.

Foot braces. Foot braces—those small pedals mounted inside the kayak—enable you to brace yourself securely in the boat. Those that can be easily adjusted with the feet are much more convenient than those that require you to reach inside the boat and do it by hand. Most boats with rudders also use the foot braces to move the rudder back and forth.

Bulkheads. Bulkheads inside the boat are needed to strengthen the deck and to aid in flotation, allowing only the cockpit to fill with water if the boat capsizes. Many plastic kayaks also have an aluminum bar that extends at least partway down the inside length of the boat's hull. This adds structural rigidity and helps prevent the inward buckling of the hull (called "oil canning").

Hatches. Hatches—lids that either screw on or are strapped on—allow you to gain access to the compartments created by the bulkheads, where you can store camping and other gear.

HISTORY OF THE BAIDARKA

The ancient *baidarka* of the Aleutians was the predecessor of the modern kayak, and its history and development make for a fascinating tale. George Dyson has done a magnificent job of tracing that story in his lavishly illustrated book *Baidarka: The Kayak* (Seattle: Alaska Northwest Books, 1986). Also of interest to kayak historians is *The Aleutian Kayak* by Wolfgang Brinck (Camden, ME: Ragged Mountain Press, 1995).

An organization has been established to preserve the legend of this fascinating skin boat. Contact the Baidarka Historical Society, P.O. Box 5454, Bellingham, WA 98227.

THE RECREATIONAL TOURING KAYAK

Casual recreational kayaks are made to be stable and therefore are easy for beginners to use. As a result, they're a little broader than most true sea kayaks, and they often have a flatter bottom as well. Most recreational boats are somewhat shorter to make them more maneuverable. The downside to all this is that they don't track (hold a straight line) as well, and they're also a little slower.

Because they're intended for less strenuous use, casual recreational boats often don't have options such as rudders or bulkhead compartments with hatches. Some have extremely large cockpits so you don't feel like you have to shoehorn yourself into them. A number of versions are even sit-on-tops, so claustrophobia is not a problem.

PERCEPTION

The range of kayak models available for touring is impressive.

INVENTION OF THE KAYAK

Over the centuries, the earliest known inhabitants of the arctic regions of North America developed a remarkable craft for traveling over icy bays, inlets, and even the open ocean. These light and fast-moving skin boats were designed primarily for hunting and fishing. Called *kayaks* by the Eskimos, they were masterpieces of primitive engineering. Made of driftwood and the skins and sinews of animals, the ancient Eskimo kayak was a remarkably resilient and durable craft, both light to handle and swift in the water. The recommended resource for kayak history is *The Bark Canoes and Skin Boats of North America* by Edwin Tappan Adney and Howard L. Chapelle (Washington, DC: Smithsonian Institute Press, 1993).

To give you a better idea of the differences between casual recreational boats and sea kayaks, let's compare two models. Old Town Canoe Company of Old Town, Maine, makes a casual recreational boat called the Loon 138. It's 13 feet, 8 inches long and made of a polyethylene called Polylink 3. It retails for about $500. Current Designs, a Canadian company in Sidney, British Columbia, makes a sea kayak called the Expedition. It's 18 feet, 10 inches long and is available in either fiberglass or Kevlar. It retails for about $2,700 or $3,200, depending on the material.

The Loon is 29½ inches wide; the Expedition is 22½ inches. The Loon weighs 54 pounds; the Expedition weighs 50 or 56 pounds, depending on the material. The cockpit on the Loon is 18 by 55 inches; the cockpit on the Expedition is 16 by 31 inches.

The Loon has a shallow V bottom and tumblehome sides (that is, the hull curves inward from the water line toward the gunwales); the Expedition has a rounded V bottom and flared sides. The Loon has a very simple deck bungee on the bow; the Expedition has more elaborate deck bungees on the bow and stern. The rudder and rear deck hatch are optional on the Loon; they're standard (and more robust) on the Expedition.

These two models may be extremes (though there are even more basic recreational boats), but you get the idea. If you were planning to paddle across the Atlantic, you'd definitely want the Expedition, but if you wanted to paddle across a small alpine lake in Idaho, the Expedition would be overkill. And, of course, the Expedition costs about six times as much. It all depends on what you plan to do with the boat.

THE SEA KAYAK

It is evident that sea kayaks are by far the most efficient and safest boats for self-propelled travel on large bodies of water such as oceans or the Great Lakes. Although open canoes have a large storage capacity, they're difficult to paddle under windy conditions and are dangerous for paddling in turbulent waters and surf. Whitewater kayaks are very stable in waves but are inefficient for distance touring and have little storage space. They're also virtually impossible to paddle under windy conditions.

For paddling on open waters where the dominant forces on the boat are wind and waves, a kayak that moves ahead efficiently and tracks in a straight line is paramount. Constant corrections to keep the boat heading on course reduce the distance traveled and waste valuable energy. In most cases, the hull should be large enough to carry camping gear and other equipment.

To increase tracking ability, you need not only a longer kayak but also one with little rocker in the bow and stern. This increases lateral resistance in the ends and prevents the kayak from easily changing direction. A longer boat travels straighter, is relatively fast, and has plenty of interior room for gear. The ultimate goal of sea kayak design, then, is to reduce the adverse effects of wind.

To reduce the effects of the wind, the height of the deck is reduced, leaving just enough room ahead of the cockpit for your knees and enough buoyancy in the bow to provide lifting motion to boost the boat over waves. (Reducing the deck height to avoid the wind can go too far, though, to the point where the boat is easily capsized by waves.) The result is a long, narrow craft capable of carrying a significant load at a good speed with the least effort, but requiring a little more attention to balance than is necessary in a casual recreational boat.

Sea kayaks are well-suited for travel on large bodies of water.

SEA KAYAK DESIGN

Sea kayakers might say that a particular model is of the West Greenland style. These boats are stable, rough-water, oceangoing boats because they are predictable and easy to roll. They have rockered (upturned) ends, chined (angled) hulls, turned-up sterns, and long, straight, and elegant bows. Their primary drawback is the lack of carrying capacity for gear, since they are designed to reduce resistance from the wind.

Sea kayaks designed in England—following in the tradition of the West Greenland style—are generally noted for their remarkable rough-weather performance. These boats have evolved along the exposed coast of the British Isles, where rough water is the rule rather than the exception. They are narrower and have more rounded hulls, but they enable a kayaker to lean into a wave if necessary, which means better secondary stability. The bow flare of these kayaks keeps them from burying their bows when surfing waves. Narrow boats with upturned ends and well-fitting cockpits can also be Eskimo-rolled more easily, if necessary, providing a kayaker with a sense of confidence.

The Pacific Northwest style of kayak, in contrast, reflects the unique conditions of that area: hundreds of miles of protected waterways, where a kayaker isn't exposed to the rigors of the open sea unless he or she

*A kayak's performance in wind and
waves is especially important in offshore paddling.*

GREAT RIVER OUTFITTERS

chooses to paddle beyond the chain of islands. Thus, these boats are often large-volume kayaks with flat midsections; high, peaked decks; large hatches; and roomy cockpits. They are very comfortable for long trips, have high initial stability, and can carry tremendous amounts of gear, but they have a high wind profile. As a result, some of them are not well suited to rough seas, and they are usually more difficult to Eskimo-roll.

There has been a tendency among some U.S. designers to adopt more characteristics of the Greenland-style kayak, which has led to a narrowing of differences between the two types of sea kayaks. For those who want to paddle along unprotected sections of coastline and do not want to be limited only to good weather in sheltered areas, the performance of a kayak in wind and waves is the most significant factor in choosing the right boat.

There are a number of points to consider when looking for the right sea kayak:

- Decide what kind of paddling you will do most (calm-water cruising, extended coastal cruising, expeditions, and so forth).
- Study as many different kayaks as possible in the appropriate class.
- Talk to as many experienced paddlers as possible about their own boats.
- Paddle the boat of your choice in as many conditions as possible.
- Assess the performance of the kayak in relation to its design, weight, materials, and cost.

Waterproof hatches allow easy access to gear.

Deck bungees are useful for holding bilge pumps, maps, and other items.

A retractable rudder has almost become standard equipment on sea kayaks.

SEA KAYAK FEATURES

If you're looking at sea kayaks, be sure to consider the following features:

Bulkheads and hatches. An important feature of sea kayaks is the fitting of watertight storage compartments with bulkheads and hatches. With watertight bulkheads, usually no additional flotation is necessary.

Rudder. Rudders are commonly made an option on kayaks, though a few boats are designed to be used without them. Rudders generally make turning the boat easier. Some boaters eschew rudders because they feel that they are a crutch for poor technique, and because they are prone to failure in severe conditions. But rudder design and materials have improved greatly in recent years, and most boaters now use them.

Retractable skeg. A skeg is a fixed, rudderlike fin under the stern of the boat, and its purpose is to increase directional stability. The skeg blade is usually enclosed in a watertight box inside the kayak's rear compartment. This almost foolproof system adds a lot of versatility to kayaks. The question of rudders on sea kayaks has always been controversial, and the skeg offers a compromise for those who are undecided.

CLASSIC SEA JOURNEYS

There are two books that every touring kayaker should have in his or her library, just for inspiration: *Seekers of the Horizon*, edited by Will Nordby (Old Saybrook, CT: Globe Pequot Press, 1989), is a collection of stories from around the world about journeys varying in length from day trips to an 8,000-mile solo expedition. *The Hidden Coast* by Joel W. Rogers (Rothell, WA: Alaska Northwest Books, 1991) is a beautiful coffee-table book, full of stunning photography, covering the western coastline from Alaska to Mexico.

Deck-fitted compass. For safety and convenience, a compass is strongly recommended as a deck fitting. Many designs allow the compass to be removed from the boat for transport.

KAYAK MATERIALS

There are several materials from which kayaks can be built. A kayak designer looks for a material that balances three elements—weight, strength, and cost— in a way that matches a clear vision of how the boat should perform.

The lighter the boat, the less water it has to displace as it moves. Naturally, this makes the boat easier to paddle. Weight, however, is often reduced at the expense of durability. With exotic materials, designers can produce a hull that is exceptionally strong and light, but the cost will be high. Strong hulls can be made from less expensive materials, but this usually means a heavier boat.

PLASTICS

Most recreational touring kayaks are made of molded polyethylene. It is inexpensive and durable, slips easily over rocks, and can be molded into complex shapes. But not all plastics are alike, and there are considerable differences in terms of strength, weight, performance, and maintenance. There are two common types of polyethylene: linear and cross-linked. Strands of linear polyethylene are very long, whereas cross-linked strands are shorter and chemically bonded to one another. Linear is easier to recycle, and cross-linked is stiffer.

To make a hull, manufacturers use one of two processes: roto-molding or blow-molding. With roto-molding (the most common method), powdered polyethylene is poured into an aluminum mold and heated until it

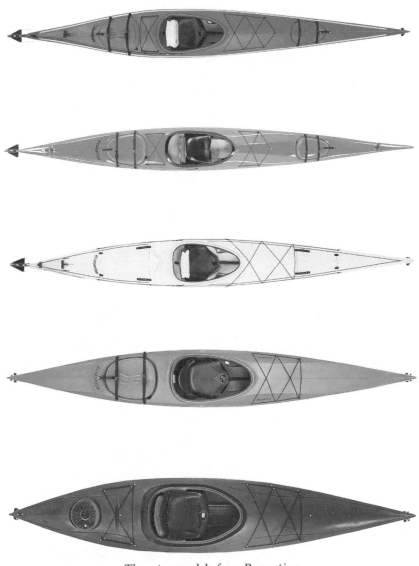

*These ten models from Perception
represent a small portion of the many shapes and styles of kayaks available.*

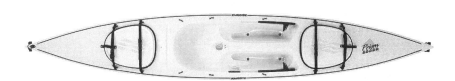

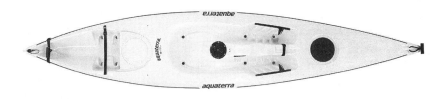

melts. The mold is then rocked and rotated until the inside is coated with a layer of molten plastic. When it cools, the plastic congeals, and a hull is born. The process takes about an hour.

Blow-molding involves feeding plastic pellets into a screw-driven extruder that produces such extreme pressure that the pellets become semimolten without additional heating. This pressure forces the molecules into a dense package. A boat-sized tube of the semimolten material emerges from the extruder, and a hydraulic ram clamps the two halves of the mold tightly over it. Air pressure is forcefully blown in through the cockpit, keeping the plastic compressed until it cools. The process produces a boat every ten minutes.

The most perceptible difference between the two methods is that a blow-molded hull is thicker, heavier, and stiffer—so stiff, in fact, that it doesn't require internal support such as foam pillars.

COMPOSITES

Some kayaks are made by fitting layers of cloth into a mold and adding resin to create a stiff, tough shell. The most common fabrics are fiberglass and the more durable Kevlar, but composites also include materials such as graphite.

A good fiberglass boat can be very tough, but it may not be durable enough for repeated whitewater use. There are several manufacturing techniques. A chopper gun lay-up refers to the process of mixing chopped glass fibers with resin and spraying it into a mold, gradually building up the hull. These boats are usually less expensive than those made of cloth; they can be durable, but quality varies.

A Kevlar boat usually weighs about 25 percent less than its fiberglass counterpart, yet with added strength. Fiberglass and Kevlar can be combined in a variety of configurations, from mat (short, chopped fibers) to roving (large bundles of fibers) to more exotic fabrics. The term "proprietary lay-up" refers to a particular manufacturer's combination of fibers and resins. Most are competitive with fiberglass in weight and cost but strive for greater durability. All these materials allow builders to create complex shapes with sharp, efficient lines. The sophistication of these materials is reflected in their high prices.

Most composite hulls have an outer layer of gel-coat resin, which protects the fabric from sunlight and abrasion and gives the hull its color and shine. Gel-coat, however, can add up to 10 pounds in weight.

OTHER MATERIALS

Though used much less frequently, a number of other materials are also available for the manufacture of touring kayaks.

Wooden kayaks. These kayaks are made of long, thin planks of wood glued together (the boats are called "strippers"). The hull is usually covered inside and out with fiberglass cloth and resin. These boats can be molded into highly complex shapes and may be very lightweight. Wooden boats are attractive, but they are also expensive and less durable than those made of plastics or composites.

Folding kayaks. These folding craft have a fabric skin of coated nylon or canvas stretched over a wooden or aluminum frame. Folding kayaks have been around since the turn of the century, and the longevity of the concept is a testament to their durability. Disassembled, a folding boat fits into two or three duffels that can be checked as luggage or stored in a closet. These boats are slightly less responsive than hard-shell kayaks, and they can be very expensive. Those interested in these boats are referred to the book *The Complete Folding Kayaker* by Ralph Diaz (Camden, ME: Ragged Mountain Press, 1994).

Inflatable kayaks. Serious paddlers used to scoff at these boats, but in recent years, inflatable canoes and kayaks have become increasingly sophisticated, and they now offer appealing designs and bombproof materials. The big advantage of inflatables, of course, is their compactness and portability. These boats perform best on whitewater and in rivers with current. Newer models are more rigid than ever but are still more sluggish on flatwater than hard-shell boats. Those interested in these boats are referred to the book *Inflatable Kayaking: The Complete Guide* (Mechanicsburg, PA: Stackpole Books, 1997).

PADDLING ASSOCIATIONS

Here are two paddling organizations worth joining:

American Canoe Association, 7432 Alban Station Blvd., Suite B-226, Springfield, VA 22150, (703) 451-0141

North American Paddlesports Association, 12455 North Wauwatosa Rd., Mequon, WI 53097, (414) 242-5228

CUSTOMIZING YOUR KAYAK

The old cliché is that one doesn't so much sit in a kayak as wear it, and this is where internal braces are helpful. Various types of hip, knee, and thigh bracing systems (made of fiberglass, plastic, or foam) are incorporated to provide the boater with a tight, secure fit.

Hip braces. The point of contact between the boat and your hips is an important balance point. Without a firm connection between your hips and the seat, you cannot effectively transfer your body movements to the boat. These braces are also necessary to do a proper Eskimo roll to the upright position.

Gluing extra foam padding to the sides of the seat where needed will make all the difference in your control of the boat. Hip pads that are thicker on their upper and stern ends provide the most secure fit.

Knee and thigh braces. Knees and thighs are responsible for much of the effectiveness of the kayaker's balancing and leaning movements. The wider you can get your knees, the better your side-to-side balancing will be. Additional padding here has two advantages: By effectively lowering the inside of the deck, it allows you to spread your knees farther apart, and it also gives you more surface area to brace against. Also, this padding is more comfortable than bare plastic. However, if you do make changes to the kayak's bracing, be sure that you can still exit the boat easily if it overturns.

Back supports. Back support is essential to both comfort and control in paddling. A back support has two functions: It transfers energy to the stroke, and it helps keep your posture upright, which is critical to the proper placement of a stroke. It also helps prevent back pain.

Many seats have a built-in back support, but if yours doesn't, there are padded nylon back straps that can be added. A back strap should be tight enough to maintain good posture but not so tight that it causes you to bend forward or makes your legs fall asleep. The back strap should cradle the small of your back, and it should be positioned so that you can get in and out of the boat easily.

Deck Bungees. This network of shock cord that is found on many touring boats holds all sorts of things to the deck. On the foredeck, these bungees typically hold your map, bilge pump, furled sail or kite, and small articles of clothing that you put on and take off as you paddle. On the aftdeck, these bungees usually hold the paddle-float attachment used for self-rescue, and farther aft is the system for attaching a spare breakdown paddle. All shock cords needs to be replaced whenever they start to lose their elasticity.

2

PADDLING ACCESSORIES

You've chosen your kayak—now you need to accessorize it. You'll need to acquire the standard paddling gear: a paddle, a life jacket, and a spray skirt. And depending on your boat and your destination, you may also need to consider a number of other accessories. (See appendix 3 for sources of accessories.)

KAYAK PADDLES

A good kayak paddle should be light, strong, and well balanced. The choice is not as easy as it first appears. Which design? Which material? Which size? The decision is an important one: After paddling hundreds, even thousands, of strokes a day, the wrong choice will be very evident to your arm and back muscles.

DESIGN
Kayak paddles can be almost as specialized as kayaks, and the final decision is largely a subjective one. You'll want to take a good look at the construction of the paddle you have in mind.

Blades—feathered or not. The first question you must answer is whether you want the blades of the paddle to be feathered or unfeathered. Unfeathered means that the two blades are in the same plane, and feathered means that the two blades are set at a right angle to each other.

The theory of a feathered blade is that when the blades are at a right angle to each other, the blade that is out of the water knifes cleanly through the air. This is no doubt a subtle advantage, but the majority of paddles are of the feathered design. The angle of the blade in feathered paddles varies somewhat from 60 to 90 degrees. A number of paddle shafts disconnect in the middle, allowing you to choose the angle.

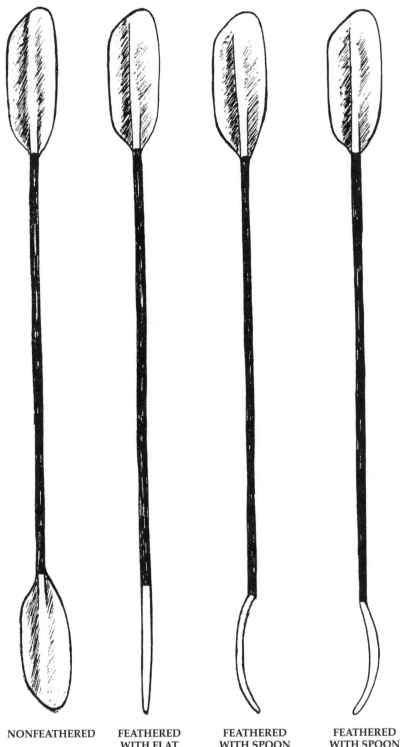

NONFEATHERED   **FEATHERED WITH FLAT BLADE**   **FEATHERED WITH SPOON BLADE (RIGHT-HAND CONTROL)**   **FEATHERED WITH SPOON BLADE (LEFT-HAND CONTROL)**

Blade shape. Blades come in two general shapes—flat or spooned. The advantage of a flat blade is that you can use either side of the paddle to paddle with. But if the blade is shaped slightly like a spoon, it grabs the water more easily and produces less cavitation in the water. Though a little troublesome to use at first, a spooned blade has advantages that are well worth the initial confusion.

The top and bottom of the blade are sometimes shaped differently to provide better energy transfer and to keep the blade more horizontal in the water. These asymmetrical blades are considerably longer than they are wide and are used mostly for long-distance cruising rather than for whitewater.

Control hand. If you use a feathered paddle with a spooned blade, you will have to specify right-hand control (by far the most common) or left-hand control. The control hand's grip never changes during paddling, although the wrist does flex. The other hand, the noncontrol, or slip, hand, loosens between strokes to allow the shaft to rotate back and forth. This technique is described more fully in chapter 5.

Blade size. Large blades are based on the theory that the more water you move, the more power you have. Most kayakers now believe that a strong stroke is a matter of blade control, not size. A slightly smaller blade is certainly preferable if you anticipate a lot of flatwater or wind. Again, the choice is largely a subjective one.

Shaft. The two choices here are round and oval. Most paddlers prefer an oval shaft because it fits more comfortably in the hands and because it's easier to orient the angle of the blade in the water. If you use a feathered paddle with spooned blades, an oval shaft makes it easier to correctly position your hands, and it gives you more control over the blade angle.

Some paddle shafts are one-piece, with the blades held in a fixed position. Others are of the breakdown variety, and their locking mechanisms allow you to choose between a feathered and an unfeathered position. These take-apart paddles are also easier to store as spares, which is a good idea on isolated trips.

Paddle shafts also come in different diameters, which may be important if you have small hands. Placing drip rings near the blades will keep your hands dry. Some paddlers secure the grip by using the same tape that tennis players wrap around their rackets.

PERCEPTION

Blades come in large and small sizes.
Which size works best is largely the paddler's choice.

MATERIALS

Paddles are made of various materials, and each has a different feel, weight, and durability. A lively debate naturally ensues among paddlers about which is the most desirable. The final decision is ultimately a subjective one.

Wood. Most wood paddles are made from strips of wood that are either glued or laminated together. Sitka spruce, western red cedar, and ash

GREAT RIVER OUTFITTERS

Paddles are made of various materials,
giving each one a different feel, weight, and durability.

are commonly used. Many of the better models are covered with a protective layer of fiberglass, and others are finished with varnish. To improve durability, the tips of wooden paddles are often reinforced with hardwood or fiberglass or capped with metal or plastic.

Wood, although beautiful and flexible, is expensive and requires frequent care. Wooden paddles, even those from the same manufacturer, may vary considerably in weight, balance, and beauty. But many paddlers feel that the pleasing flexibility of a wood paddle can't be duplicated in a synthetic material. Wood shafts also feel warmer in cold weather.

Synthetics. Fabrics such as Kevlar, graphite, and carbon fiber are light and strong, but they're expensive. Fiberglass is durable, has good flex, and is moderately priced. Blades are thin and slice well through the water. Some surprisingly good, yet relatively inexpensive, paddles are made with fiberglass blades and aluminum shafts. Carbon fiber is lighter, stiffer, and a little more durable than fiberglass. Fiberglass-reinforced polypropylene appears to be the material of choice for durable, performance-oriented economy paddles. These blades are very stiff and durable.

SIZE

There's no easy rule for selecting paddle length, but it's important nonetheless. The optimal length depends on your height, the length of your arms, and your preferred style of paddling. The paddle must be suited to your boat. Wide kayaks, particularly wide tandem boats, usually require the longest paddles available to allow you to reach the water without hitting the deck or shifting the paddle from side to side. The height of your torso in relation to the depth of the cockpit and deck shape also affects what you need; for example, a short-waisted person in a deep boat requires a longer paddle.

Paddles are typically sold in centimeter lengths. The length you'll need depends on the type of paddling you'll be doing. The most popular sizes seem to be those between 7½ and 8 feet (228 and 244 centimeters). For wider, tandem kayaks, many paddlers prefer longer, 8½-foot (258 centimeters) paddles.

If you like to paddle at a slow cadence, you'll be happier with a longer paddle. If you like to paddle at a brisk clip, you might consider a shorter paddle. Either way, touring kayakers should try to maintain their stroke speed to protect their arms, especially when paddling upwind. As a result, the trend has been toward shorter paddles or narrower blades. If you're undecided between two sizes, select the shorter one, and if possible, try it before you buy it.

DRIP RINGS

The rubber drip rings on the shaft of the paddle are very helpful when touring. They prevent water from running down the shaft onto your hands, and they also make the water drip from the paddle far enough to the sides to keep the water from dripping on your arms.

PADDLE LEASH

Losing your paddle is something to avoid at all costs. A paddle leash, made from a ³⁄₁₆- to ¼-inch line or elastic cord, can be used to connect the paddle to your wrist or your boat's deck bungees. Keep the leash long enough to slide between your hands on the paddle shaft so that you can still roll and brace.

SPARE PADDLE

Even with a paddle leash, a spare paddle is essential in all but the most tame situations. Though breaking a paddle is rare with today's materials, it does happen occasionally. Losing a paddle is much more likely, from either a capsize or a high tide that unexpectedly floods your campsite.

Some boaters use a short, single-bladed, bent-shaft canoe paddle for a spare. If you use a double-blade paddle as a spare, it must be a breakdown model. Most kayakers store them on the rear deck for easy access from the cockpit, and a number of kayaks have deck rigging for that purpose. You might consider buying a spare paddle that complements your primary paddle—perhaps one with a different-sized blade or one of a different length—for a change of pace or conditions.

GEAR UPDATE

The specifications of all touring kayaks on the market and their related gear can be found in the annual buyers' guide in the December issue of *Canoe & Kayak* magazine. This is an invaluable resource for gear-obsessed paddlers of all types.

LIFE JACKETS

Few pieces of boating gear have progressed more in comfort and safety than the life jacket. Personal flotation devices, or PFDs, as they're called by the Coast Guard, can generally be described by their type.

There are many models of Type III PFDs on the market made especially for kayakers. They are usually shorter and have flotation "ribs" rather than "slabs" to accommodate kayakers' need for more freedom of motion. Type V includes special designs for whitewater, generally with commercial raft passengers in mind. These jackets often provide greater flotation and safety than Type III, but they tend to be too big and restrictive for kayakers. (Incidentally, Type I is the bulky orange "Mae West" jacket often filled with kapok; Type II is the horse-collar version, which is inadequate for river use; and Type IV is a buoyant seat cushion, unsuitable for just about everything.)

There are a number of life jackets designed specifically for touring kayakers.

**PERSONAL FLOTATION
DEVICE (PFD)**

When choosing a PFD, favor safety over comfort. PFDs designed for kayakers often have extra flotation in the area below the waist, and this band of flotation can be flipped up for more comfort. The amount of flotation you require in a life jacket depends primarily on your body's own flotation, your experience, and the kind of water you'll be tackling.

For easy rivers and small lakes, a "shorty" version of a Type III PFD offers a good measure of safety and unrestricted motion. When paddling large bodies of water, a high-flotation version of a Type III is better yet. There should be sufficient buckles and straps to secure the jacket firmly around your body, and you should always fasten all buckles, zippers, and waist ties when you put the life jacket on. The PFD should fit snugly to keep it from riding up over your head. *Never* wear the PFD loose or open in the front. This is also important to avoid entangling yourself should the boat overturn. Make a habit of securing your life jacket when you take it off, so the wind doesn't blow it away.

PERCEPTION

WAVE PFD

A good PFD will give you years of service if treated properly. Don't use your life jacket as a seat cushion. After each trip, hang the jacket to maintain its shape and prevent it from mildewing. Clean it often, using a mild soap so as not to harm the interior foam.

SPRAY SKIRTS

A spray skirt serves a number of functions. It keeps wind-whipped waves from splashing into the cockpit, and in a capsize, it keeps water out of the boat so that you can

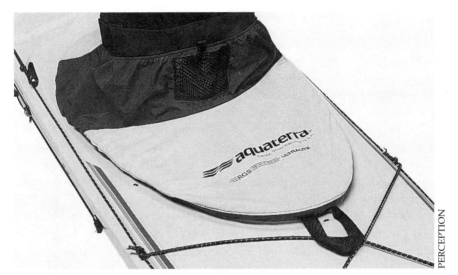

PERCEPTION

Spray skirt attached to a kayak.

execute an Eskimo roll. The spray skirt also keeps your body warm and dry while you're paddling.

Spray skirts have four basic features: the tubular skirt that fits around the paddler, the deck that covers the cockpit, a grab loop at the front of the skirt for quick removal, and an elastic cord around the bottom of the cover to help seal it watertight. Some models have suspenders.

Most spray skirts are made from either coated nylon or neoprene. The nylon ones are good for moderate conditions, are very durable, and are less expensive. Some have an adjustable drawstring at the waist, which is a handy feature. Neoprene covers keep out water better and keep you warmer, which may be a disadvantage in warm weather. Many spray skirts use an elastic cord to attach the skirt to the boat, but those with an elastic band fit more tightly.

The spray skirt must fit you and your boat snugly but not too tightly, lest it constrict your movements. When you're deciding what size spray skirt to buy, factor in the extra thickness that cold-weather clothing will add. The spray skirt should also have enough flexibility that it will slip off the cockpit if you draw your knees up and push yourself away from the kayak. Try this a couple of times to satisfy yourself that the spray skirt will detach when you need it to.

BILGE PUMPS

A bilge pump is used to remove water from a kayak, and it's especially important after the capsize of a solo paddler who has few other means of getting the water out. Bilge pumps are of two types: electric or manual (handheld or mounted on the deck).

Compact, lightweight, battery-powered pumps developed for sea kayaks can bail out a boat rapidly while the boater continues to paddle. This is the most expensive alternative, and it requires that you keep the batteries charged, though solar cells are available. It also adds more weight to the boat.

Handheld manual pumps (usually plastic and about 18 inches long and 2 inches in diameter) are by far the most popular option, largely because they are inexpensive and lightweight. To keep the pump from floating away, you need to tether it to the boat or make sure it's secured under the deck bungees.

Deck-mounted manual pumps with a lever action are also available. They allow you to pump with one hand while the spray skirt remains in place, but they do not move the water as fast as handheld pumps and are heavier.

Regardless of the pump you use, a large sponge is good for sopping up the small amount of water that inevitably comes in through the spray skirt.

A deck-mounted bilge pump doesn't require removal of the spray skirt.

BILGE PUMP

COMPASSES

Every kayaker should carry a compass on anything beyond a backyard trip. The choices are a small, inexpensive hiker's compass or the bulkier, more costly marine compass. A hiker's compass works fine, but the marine compass is more convenient and easier to use. With a marine compass, you can take bearings on a landscape feature in the distance and simply point the boat toward it. Doing the same with a hiker's compass requires that you stop paddling and adjust the compass.

DECK-MOUNTED
COMPASS

Marine compasses offer other advantages. They are gimballed to accommodate boat movement, and a compass light makes night paddling and navigation easier. If mounted permanently, the marine compass adds weight to the boat and is vulnerable to damage during boat handling. Some models, however, can be dismounted from the kayak while the boat is in transport.

PADDLE FLOATS

The paddle float, an inflatable bag that fits on the blade of the paddle, makes a stabilizing outrigger to help a boater reenter the boat after a capsize. This device is very effective, easy to stow on board, and relatively inexpensive. A paddle float is especially important if you paddle alone. If you paddle in groups, assisted recoveries may be more appropriate, and the float becomes less critical.

PADDLE FLOAT

FLOTATION BAGS

For safety reasons, every kayak should have flotation at both ends, provided by either bulkhead compartments or flotation bags. The safest system of all is to have both, just in case the hatches or bulkheads leak. For day trips in boats without bulkheads, simple inflatable air bags work fine. For longer trips, some flotation in the same space where gear is stored is required.

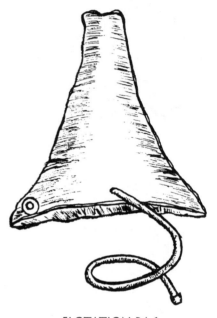

Most paddlers choose to rely on their bulkhead compartments to provide buoyancy when the boat is loaded with camping gear. In boats without bulkheads, gear can be enclosed in flotation bags that are filled with gear and then inflated. The flotation bags should be secured in place to prevent them from popping out when the kayak is swamped.

If you decide to take an empty boat out for the day during a long trip, be sure to insert flotation bags where the gear was. Likewise, if

FLOTATION BAG

your flotation system typically works only with a large amount of gear, buy flotation bags that will work alone, so you will have the added buoyancy if you need it.

WATERPROOF BAGS

Waterproof bags are used primarily to keep things dry. Unlike flotation bags, they cannot be inflated to fill spaces. Nonetheless, putting as much gear as possible into dry bags, whether it needs protection or not, adds buoyancy if the boat is swamped.

Bags constructed of thicker material last longer, as the abrasion from sliding the bags in and out of the boat quickly wears through thinner ones. Most bags seal with a roll-down top and secure by bending the roll and clipping the ends together. They are waterproof when the top is rolled down three or four times and then bent away from the direction of rolling for clipping. It's important not to overfill the bag so that there is room left for sealing.

The smallest size makes a good day bag, which can be placed between the knees to hold things that might be needed while paddling—sunglasses, compass, small binoculars or camera, sunscreen, or snacks. Medium sizes are handy for sleeping bags, spare clothes, or food. Generally, it's better to use small and medium-sized bags rather than large ones so that you can fill all the spaces effectively.

Unless you carry a waterproof or water-resistant camera, your camera should be carried in a waterproof bag or box when not in use. Waterproof camera bags

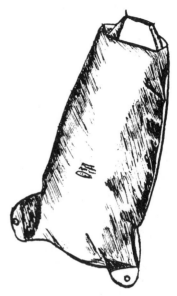

WATERPROOF BAG

are the most compact, but they are a bit cumbersome to open and close. Plastic waterproof boxes are available, as well as surplus ammunition boxes, which are easy to open and close but a little bulky.

SEA SOCKS

Boaters attempting long open crossings often use sea socks. A sea sock is a large coated-nylon bag that fits into the cockpit and is fitted over the cockpit coaming to limit the amount of water that can enter the boat. You sit inside the sock and put your spray skirt on the coaming over it.

Sea socks should never replace other means of buoyancy such as bulkheads or flotation bags, but they do reduce the water volume entering the boat in a capsize. Tandem kayaks in particular can take on an enormous amount of water when swamped.

WEATHER RADIOS

Continuous VHF (very high frequency) weather broadcasts are provided for most coastal regions and many large inland waters by the National Oceanic and Atmospheric Administration (NOAA) in the United States and by the Coast Guard in Canada. You can use a multiband radio that

PADDLERS' TALES

This report comes from Dave Gardner about paddling Britain's Shetland Islands:

"The venue was Papa Stour, a small island off the west coast of Shetland—reputed to have the best sea caves in Britain. We spent the weekend paddling around the coastline of Papa Stour visiting the remarkable caves, subterranean passages, and natural arches. On Sunday, three of the group paddled across to the Ve Skeffies. This journey, though only about 5 miles, is across an area subjected to tide races and overfalls, plus very confused tidal streams. On Monday, we paddled back across Papa Sound to 'mainland' Shetland. This crossing requires a bit of planning, as the tide runs at 6 knots and there are a few small overfalls.

"Two of our group set off for another four days of paddling around Shetland. During their travels they landed on the isle of Muckle Flugga—the most northerly island of Britain—and had tea with the lighthouse keeper. I understand he was quite surprised by their arrival, as they don't get many visitors there. The next day, while camping at Urie Ness on the Isle of Fetiar, Mike and Bill saw a pod of killer whales feeding on seals just offshore from their tent."

includes a weather band or a small, inexpensive weather radio that tunes only to these frequencies. Handheld marine VHF transceivers pick up all weather frequencies and often receive them clearly when other radios cannot. For more information on these radios, see chapter 7.

GLOBAL POSITIONING SYSTEMS

A global positioning system (GPS) is a small, handheld, battery-operated electronic device that can pinpoint your position anywhere on earth within a hundred yards or so. Many boaters find that it relieves the tedium of trying to constantly determine their location with a compass, and for long open crossings, it is especially useful.

The GPS works in conjunction with satellites that send out signals that are captured by the device's receiver. The screen on the GPS gives you a reading of your longitude and latitude. GPSs come in varying levels of sophistication and accuracy, but a number of inexpensive and reliable models are now available. Like all electronic devices, though, they can fail, so a compass should always be carried as a backup.

EMERGENCY SIGNALING DEVICES

A number of emergency signaling devices are available for those kayakers who take trips into remote areas or dangerous waters where rescue may depend on outside assistance. Obviously, only very experienced paddlers should attempt trips that require this equipment. These devices are covered in more detail in chapter 8.

VISUAL DISTRESS SIGNALS
There are many options that vary in price and effectiveness. These include flares, strobe lights, and signal mirrors.

VHF RADIOS
Handheld marine VHF radios are generally the most effective emergency signaling devices, and most have a range of 5 to 10 miles. Once the Coast Guard receives your call for help, rescue helicopters can follow your signal as long as you keep pushing the transmit button periodically.

EMERGENCY POSITION-INDICATING RADIO BEACONS
The advantage of emergency position-indicating radio beacons (EPIRBs) over VHF radios is that, once activated, they transmit a special beep continuously and automatically for up to twenty-four hours. They can only transmit a beep, however; they cannot receive or transmit voice.

DOWN TO BAJA

The 800-mile Baja California coast is legendary among kayakers for its dolphins, its giant winged manta rays, its crimson tides, and its relentless wind. Jonathan Waterman and his wife spent two months among the tides and storms that define the legendary sea of Cortez. The results of those experiences are detailed in a provocatively written series of essays titled *Kayaking the Vermillion Sea* (New York: Simon & Schuster, 1995).

SAILS AND KITES

You certainly do not need a sail or a kite for touring, but they can add speed and are great fun on breezy days. Specialized kayak sails and cloth parafoil kites are available commercially. Both sails and kites have advantages and disadvantages, depending on the circumstances. Sails are more useful than kites in light winds, but kites are safer in strong winds because they have less tipping force.

There are a variety of kayak sail rigs on the market. They vary greatly in size, and the best ones allow paddling while under sail (otherwise, in light winds, you end up going slower). Most masts are placed in a hole in the hull or against the front of the coaming. A kite designed for cruising can be handheld, but you should be able to tie it off to the deck, while still ensuring that it is quickly releasable.

Some sail designs allow sailing upwind, but trying to go upwind makes little sense for touring. Windward sailing requires bulky leeboards and outriggers, greatly increases the risk of a capsize, and is usually slower than paddling.

There are a variety of sail rigs available.

CARTOP RACKS

Touring kayaks, because of their size and shape, are best transported with cartop racks designed especially to secure them. These racks not only are safer and more secure, but they also prevent the caving in of the hull (called "oil canning") that can occur with plastic boats. They can also be used to transport paddles, camping equipment, and other gear. These racks can be quite expensive, but the range of designs and accessories is impressive. A number of excellent racks, with accessories just for kayaks, are made by Thule and Yakima Products (see appendix 3).

BOAT CARTS

Small wheeled boat carts are handy whenever you need to transport a kayak any distance by hand, especially when you have a load of gear inside. These carts are indispensable for those traveling on a ferry without a car. They're also useful for transporting the boat from the parking lot to the launch site.

There are a number of designs. Some fit on the end of the boat, others in the center. Most carts disassemble or collapse for storage in the boat or on deck. The wheels are the bulkiest item to store, so the trade-off in size is between bulk and the ability to traverse rough or soft ground.

EQUIPMENT CHECKLIST

This checklist is just a suggestion. Although some of these items are not necessary on every outing, you may want to consider carrying them for safety or comfort, depending on the destination and conditions. Some items are optional and depend on your preferences.

Kayak	Camp clothing
Paddle and spare	Camp shoes
PFD	Wallet and keys
Helmet	Waterproof bags
Tow or rescue rope	Tent or bivouac shelter
Full repair kit	Sleeping bag
Full first-aid kit	Air mattress or pad
Bilge pump/sponge	Food
Water bottle	Cookware and kitchen gear
Sunscreen	Camp stove

Clothing suitable for conditions
Footgear
Emergency supplies
Water containers
Map, guidebook
Toilet paper
Plastic trowel

Fuel
Flashlight
Insect repellent
Garbage bags
Signaling devices
Camera, fishing gear
Toiletries

3

CLOTHING

When it comes to clothing, the experts agree: Buy the best, and scrimp somewhere else. Your comfort in the wilds is too important to do otherwise. The prime purpose of clothing is to keep you warm and dry on the water, but it must do the same in camp. With the new clothing designed specifically for kayaking, there's no reason to be wet and cold.

COLD-WEATHER PADDLING

In warm weather, you can wear just about anything and get away with it. Quick-drying fabrics are more comfortable, which rules out denim jeans, and clothing made just for paddlers is widely available in outdoor stores and from catalogs. Almost ubiquitous footwear among kayakers is the river sandal, with literally dozens of styles to choose from.

The importance of proper clothing cannot be overstated.

It's easy for clothing to work if you're sitting still on a calm, dry day. But maintaining the body's temperature is difficult when you alternate sitting with varying degrees of activity in a range of temperatures and conditions. This is because an active body pumps out heat and moisture, which have to be dispersed. The body loses heat in four ways, and these determine how clothing must function.

Convection. Convection, the transfer of heat from the body to the air, is the major cause of heat loss. When air moves over the skin and through your clothing, it robs warmth at an amazing rate. Clothing must reduce airflow over the skin; in other words, it must be windproof.

Conduction. Conduction is the transfer of heat from one surface to another. Air conducts heat poorly, so the best protection is clothing that traps and holds air. It's the still air that keeps you warm—the clothing just holds it in place.

Evaporation. During vigorous exercise, the body gives off as much as a quart of water an hour. Clothing must transport it away quickly so that it doesn't absorb body heat. Wearing garments that can be ventilated easily, especially at the neck, is important.

Radiation. Radiation is the passing of heat between two objects without warming the intervening space. Radiation requires a direct pathway, so wearing tightly woven clothing solves most of the problem of loss of body heat.

LAYERING

The usual solution to the clothing dilemma is to wear several light layers of clothing on the torso and arms; the legs require less protection. These layers can then be adjusted to suit the prevailing conditions and your level of activity. Layering is versatile and efficient if used properly, which means constantly opening and closing zippers and cuff fastenings, and occasionally stopping to remove or put on clothes.

A typical layering wardrobe consists of an inner layer of thin material to remove moisture from the skin, a thicker mid-layer to trap air and provide insulation, and an outer shell to keep off wind and rain while allowing perspiration to pass through. A basic three-layer system includes a synthetic undershirt; a pile, fleece, or wool mid-layer; and a breathable, waterproof shell.

To this may be added a synthetic, wool, or cotton shirt or sweater, and perhaps a down- or synthetic-insulation-filled garment if it's really cold. If the weather will be wet as well as cold, another pile or fleece jacket can substitute for the insulation-filled garment.

How many layers to take depends on the conditions you expect. You should take clothing that will keep you warm in the worst weather you're likely to encounter. If in doubt, take a light synthetic-insulated vest, just in case.

Synthetics. If there's the slightest chance you'll get wet—and there usually is—the obvious advantage of synthetic fabrics is their ability to dry quickly. Because of this, polypropylene or polyester underwear, as well as pile and fleece insulation, works well. The effectiveness of these materials is largely dependent on their thickness. They are also extremely rugged and require little care. The only drawback is their bulk: They don't compress well for packing.

Underwear. If the weather or water turns really cold, you'll need long underwear. Polypropylene is popular because it keeps moisture off the skin. Polyester fabrics, under trade names such as Capilene, have been introduced because they pill less and remain softer than polypropylene. Even though polypropylene and polyester don't offer much insulation, the body is warmer when it's dry. Different thicknesses are now available for diverse situations.

In even colder weather, you can add additional insulating layers of pile or fleece, or you can use a thicker synthetic fill that feels like down. For use on the water, down is useless, because it takes days to dry. Wool is a good insulator when wet, although it becomes heavy, stretches, and is slow to dry. With the new synthetics, wool has lost most of its appeal.

Shell. Regardless of inner layers, a waterproof outer layer—a raincoat, paddling jacket, or dry suit—is necessary to keep the inner layers dry and to prevent heat loss. According to the experts, wool is hardly warmer than cotton unless you cover it with a shell.

Paddling jackets should allow a full range of motion.

Recognizing the advantages of a waterproof shell, kayakers were the first to develop the paddling jacket with its tight-fitting closures. There are numerous models available, but be sure to select one that fits well. It is especially important to have a full range of motion when your arms are extended so that you don't feel constrained when paddling. Your jacket should fit over your spray skirt and be cinched fairly tightly to keep water out.

The logical extension of a paddling jacket is a pair of paddling pants, complete with neoprene ankle cuffs or dry-suit seals. As with jackets, there are many models and styles on the market.

Wet suits. A neoprene wet suit is commonly used in frigid conditions, because the thin layer of water trapped underneath is warmed by the body's heat. You will not be perfectly dry in a wet suit, but if it fits properly, you will be very comfortable. Anytime the water is below 50 degrees F., a wet suit (or dry suit, if you prefer) should be worn.

Wet suit designs range from complete coverage to vest tops and shorts. Your choice should be guided by the conditions you expect to encounter and your personal toleration of cold. The standard wet suit consists of a long-sleeved jacket and pants, but the problem is that wet suit jackets are very restrictive for paddling and will quickly exhaust you. The "Farmer John" model is more popular. It covers the legs and torso but is sleeveless. Worn with a paddling jacket, it affords unrestricted movement. The "shorty" model is cut off just above the knees and is sleeveless, offering good mobility while keeping the torso warm.

One-eighth-inch-thick neoprene is the most popular for paddlers, because it provides enough protection and warmth while offering good flexibility. Suits with glued seams cost more, but they don't leak and therefore keep you warmer.

Dry suits. A coated nylon dry suit—with its looser body and its tight-fitting vinyl seals at neck, wrist, and ankles—allows insulation to be worn underneath. Many boaters find dry suits more comfortable than wet suits, but dry suits are also more expensive and more difficult to maintain than wet suits.

WET SUIT

Dry suits come in one-piece and two-piece styles. Their rubber gaskets and waterproof zippers keep you dry, even when doing an Eskimo roll. Both styles are equally waterproof, but the two-piece suits give you the option of wearing just the top when the temperature is too warm for a full dry suit. With any dry suit, be sure to keep the latex seals well lubricated to prolong their life.

Extremities. Don't forget the extremities—head, hands, feet. The head is a critical area of heat loss, since over half the body's heat can be lost there. Any type of hat will help, but in cold weather, a close-fitting wool or synthetic cap provides more warmth.

Synthetic gloves retain warmth when wet, but neoprene ones are warmer, though they can be tiring to use because of the material's tendency to spring back to its original shape. Even in warm water, many kayakers find gloves useful to prevent blisters. A device called a pogie is also effective for keeping the hands warm. It is a piece of nylon or neoprene that fits over the hand and the paddle shaft like an oversize mitten. Its advantage is that it

DRY TOP

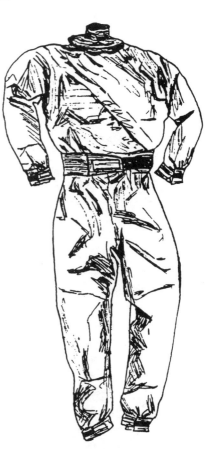

DRY SUIT

NEOMITTS (POGIES)

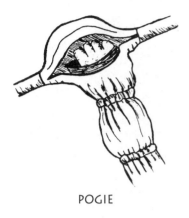

POGIE

allows you to grip the shaft with your bare hands yet keep cold water off. The pogie is cut in such a way that the fabric is wrapped around the fingers and attached with a Velcro fastener. This fastener pulls away should you need to take your hand off the paddle.

Wet suit boots (with hard soles) and wet suit socks (without) are the best protection against cold water sloshing around the bottom of the boat. A thin polypropylene liner-sock underneath will keep your feet drier and therefore warmer. Wet suit boots and shoes made just for kayakers have become increasingly sophisticated, with zippers, lace-up tops, padded insoles, and traction soles.

INNER LAYER

Often described as thermal underwear, this layer keeps the skin dry rather than warm. If perspiration is quickly removed from the skin's surface, it's easier for the outer layer to keep you warm. Conversely, if the layer next to your skin becomes saturated and dries slowly, your other clothes, no matter how good, will have a hard time keeping you warm. No fabric, regardless of its claims, can keep you warm when it is wet.

While on the move, you can stay warm even if your inner layer is damp, as long as your outer layer keeps out rain and wind and your mid-layer provides some warmth. But once you stop, wet underwear will chill you rapidly. Once you stop exercising, your heat output drops rapidly, just when you need it to dry out your wet underwear.

The material to avoid at all costs is cotton, because it absorbs moisture quickly and takes a long time to dry. To make matters worse, it clings to the skin, preventing a dry layer of air from forming.

Fabrics remove moisture in two ways. Either they transport, or "wick," moisture away from the skin and into the air or to the next layer of clothing, or they absorb it before slowly passing it to the other side. Wicking is done by specially developed synthetic materials; traditional, natural fibers absorb moisture.

You may have to wear undergarments for days without washing them, so they must work for a long time and, ideally, not absorb odors. Some of the synthetics come in heavier weights for colder conditions, but they don't wick moisture as fast as the more lightweight versions.

Designs are simple: short- and long-sleeved crew-neck tops, long-sleeved zip-neck tops, and long pants. Close-fitting garments wick moisture quicker, and mid-layers fit easily over them. Wrist and ankle cuffs need to grip well to keep them from riding up. Seams should be flat-sewn, not raised, to avoid rubbing and abrasion. Dark colors are best, because dirt and stains show up less. Check the laundering instructions: Underwear requiring special care should be avoided.

Choosing a synthetic fabric for underwear can be difficult because there are so many brands, all claiming to be best. The three main choices are polypropylene, polyester, and polyvinyl chloride (PVC).

Polypropylene. Polypropylene is the lightest and thinnest of these fabrics. It won't absorb moisture, but instead wicks it along its fibers and into the air or to the next layer. When you stop exercising, it wicks away your sweat so fast that after-exercise chill is negligible. However, polypropylene absorbs odors and doesn't smell fresh after a day or so, and it shrinks when washed in hot water. If you don't wash it every couple of days, it ceases to work properly. As a result, you have to carry several garments or rinse one out regularly. Newer versions of polypropylene have a softer, less "plastic" feel, and they can be washed at higher temperatures.

Polyester. Polyester repels water but has a low wicking ability. However, it can be treated chemically so that the surface absorbs water while the core repels it; the result is that moisture spreads over the material and quickly dries. Most versions contain an antibacterial treatment to prevent odor buildup. Unlike polypropylene, it can be washed at relatively high temperatures.

PVC. Like polypropylene and polyester, PVC absorbs little water and wicks well. It's comfortable and efficient, but it shrinks drastically if put in

---

PROFILE: DON STARKELL

Don Starkell is a man possessed. In 1980, he canoed the 12,281 miles from Winnipeg to the mouth of the Amazon, a journey chronicled in his book *Paddle to the Amazon: The Ultimate 12,000-Mile Canoe Adventure* (Toronto: McCleland & Stewart, 1995). In 1990, at the age of fifty-seven, he began a 3,200-mile kayak trip from Hudson Bay through the Northwest Passage. The trek took three summers, and the diary of that trip from Churchill, Manitoba, north and then west to Tuktoyaktuk, near Alaska, is titled *Paddle to the Arctic* (Toronto: McCleland & Stewart, 1996). It is a fascinating read, full of drama as Starkell races against the winter to finish the journey—and save his life.

water hotter than lukewarm. PVC isn't as bad as old-style polypropylene, but it retains body odor after a few days' wear. For strength, it's usually blended with nylon or polyester in an 80 percent–20 percent mix.

Wool. Wool, the traditional material, is not as popular as it once was, yet it has much to recommend it. Rather than rapidly wicking moisture, wool works more slowly, absorbing moisture to leave a dry surface against the skin. Relatively lightweight, it can absorb up to 35 percent of its weight in water before it feels wet and cold. Once wet, it's slow to dry. Many people, however, find it to be too itchy. Wool's other limitation is its warmth, which makes it suitable only for colder weather.

MID-LAYER

The mid-layer traps air and keeps you warm. Mid-layer clothing has to deal with body moisture it receives from the inner layer, so it needs to either wick that moisture away or absorb it without losing its insulation.

Mid-layer clothing comes in every design imaginable: shirts, sweaters, anoraks, and jackets. High collars keep your neck warm and hold in heat, and garments that open down the front are easier to ventilate than crewneck ones. There are a number of materials to choose from.

A SHORTSLEEVE
PADDLING SHIRT

PERCEPTION

Synthetic thermal. You can wear two layers of thin thermal underwear, but most manufacturers offer it in heavier versions, which make good mid-layers.

Wool and cotton. The traditional alternative to a synthetic fabric is wool or cotton. Wool is heavy and bulky and takes forever to dry. Cotton, too, is heavy and dries slowly. Both have become less attractive when compared with pile and fleece.

Pile and fleece. Pile and fleece insulate well, wick moisture quickly, and are lightweight, hard-wearing, warm when wet, and fast-drying. This makes them ideal for kayak camping. They can be worn over a wide temperature range—without a shell when it's warm or calm, and with one when it's cold and windy.

There are many different types and weights of pile and fleece. Pile is generally a loosely knit fabric with a furry surface, and fleece is tightly knit with a smooth finish. Manufacturers do not always use these terms consistently. Most pile and fleece are made from polyester, but a few are made from nylon; neither has any particular advantages over the other.

Worn over a synthetic inner layer and under a breathable waterproof shell, a pile or fleece top will keep you warm in just about any weather. Pile is most effective in cold, wet conditions, where other materials don't work well. A pile top can wick moisture almost as fast as synthetic underwear. If you feel cold, nothing will keep you as warm as a pile top, even a damp one.

Pile does have its drawbacks. Most garments are not windproof, which means that you need to wear a shell over them, even in a cool breeze. Shelled jackets are available, but they're heavier, bulkier, and not as versatile. Pile's biggest disadvantage is that it doesn't compress well.

Pile garments need to be close fitting to trap warm air efficiently and to wick moisture away quickly. They are prone to the bellows effect, in which cold air sucked in at the bottom of the garment replaces warm air, so the hem should be elasticized or have a draw cord. Wrist cuffs work best if they're close fitting, as do neck closures. The broad, stretchy ribbing found on the cuffs and hems of many jackets works well, but it absorbs moisture and takes a long time to dry; the nonabsorbent and quick-drying Lycra is better.

Most pile garments are hip length, which is just about right. Low, hand-warming pockets are useful.

Insulated clothing. When a pile or fleece garment won't keep you warm on its own, you need an additional insulating layer. This could be a second, perhaps thicker, pile garment, but many campers prefer down-filled clothing, which is warmer than pile, more compact, and more windproof. Down is still the lightest, warmest insulation there is, and it provides more warmth for its weight than pile. Down, however, must be kept dry; when it's wet, it loses its insulating ability, and it dries very slowly.

If you're allergic to feathers or worried about garments that won't work when wet, consider high-loft polyester-filled jackets. They're cold when wet, but they dry quickly. They are, however, bulkier than pile and down garments.

Another alternative is the thin microfiber insulations that dominate ski wear because of their slim looks. First in the field was Thinsulate, and there are now others. They're made from very fine polyester and polypropylene fibers that trap more air than any material, including down. They are, however, bulky to pack, and they dry more slowly than pile and fleece.

OUTER LAYER

If the outer layer fails, it doesn't matter how good your inner garments are. Wet clothing exposed to the wind causes a chill regardless of the material it's made from. The basic choices in outerwear are between breathable and nonbreathable fabrics.

Breathable fabrics. The moisture given off by your body eventually reaches the outer layer. If it can't escape, it condenses on the inner surface of the rain shell and eventually soaks back into your clothes. The solution is fabrics that allow water vapor to pass through while keeping the rain out. These breathable fabrics are referred to as moisture-vapor permeable (MVP); the best known is Gore-Tex. Since the advent of Gore-Tex, a number of waterproof fabrics claiming to transmit moisture vapor have appeared.

Breathable garments need to be close fitting to keep the air inside as warm as possible, because this enables the fabric to work more effectively. However, opening the front or undoing wrist fastenings is still the quickest and most efficient way to vent moisture.

Breathable fabrics aren't perfect, of course. There's a limit to the amount of moisture that even the best fabric can transmit in a given time. This means that when you exert yourself and perspire heavily, you won't be completely dry; nor will you be dry in a continuously heavy rain. When the outside of any garment is running with water, breathability is reduced, and condensation forms. In a nonbreathable garment, condensation forms until you take it off, so you stay wet even after it's stopped raining. With the best breathable fabrics, once your activity slows down and you produce less moisture, any dampness will dry out through the fabric. The same happens after a heavy rain.

There are two categories of breathable materials: coatings and laminates. Coatings are layers of waterproofing (usually polyurethane) applied to a base fabric (usually nylon). Laminates are sandwiches of materials, with the key layer consisting of a very thin, waterproof, breathable membrane. Coated fabrics, such as Entrant, are popular, and new ones are appearing. None breathe as well as the laminates, but they're an improvement over nonbreathable coatings, and the best ones work very well.

Laminates, such as Gore-Tex, are the most effective (and most expensive) breathable fabrics. Their microporous membrane can be laminated to a range of fabrics—mostly nylons, but sometimes polyester or polyester-cotton blends. The thicker the fabric, the more durable the garment, but the lower its breathability. In three-layer laminates, the membrane is glued between two layers of nylon to produce a hard-wearing but somewhat stiff material. More breathable but less durable are two-layer laminates, in which the membrane is stuck to an outer layer and the inner lining hangs free, and drop liners, in which the membrane is left loose between an inner and outer layer.

Nonbreathable fabrics. Rain gear is made from nylon coated with polyurethane or neoprene. Polyurethane is cheaper than neoprene, but it eventually cracks and peels. Neoprene is extremely hard-wearing. Both leave you soaked in sweat after exercising, and the only way to remove that moisture is to ventilate the jacket—hardly practical if it's pouring.

PADDLING JACKET

While moving, you'll still feel warm, even if your undergarments are wet with sweat, because nonbreathable rainwear holds in heat with the moisture. Because rain is colder than perspiration, it's better to wear a nonbreathable waterproof shell than a breathable nonwaterproof one. When you stop exercising, however, you'll cool down rapidly unless you put on dry clothes.

Design. Material alone is not enough to ensure that a garment is waterproof. Design is almost as crucial. Sealed seams are critical for ensuring maximum waterproofness. In breathable garments and the more expensive nonbreathable ones, the seams are tape-sealed. In cheaper garments, they may be coated with sealant instead. If you have a garment with uncoated seams, or if the sealant wears off, you can buy the sealant and coat them yourself.

Sleeves must be cut full under the arms to allow for free movement and to keep them from riding up. The cuffs should be adjustable. Simple, external, Velcro-closed ones are preferable to the more awkward internal storm cuffs; nonadjustable elasticized ones will make your arms overheat.

Pockets are undoubtedly useful, but making them waterproof is difficult. An advantage of pullover garments is that they usually have a single large "kangaroo" pouch on the chest that is easy to use and water-resistant.

4

TRIP PLANNING

The paddling trip had been planned for months, and we would soon be leaving on a two-week kayaking journey through the hinterlands. The last-minute details remained, as they always do, but the trip would ultimately justify our efforts. It always does.

THE MASTER PLAN

An extended kayak trip naturally involves a great deal of planning and provisioning if things are to go smoothly. Find out how long it normally takes to make the trip and adapt this to your plans. Give yourself plenty of leeway. The actual time will depend on many factors, such as the direction of the winds and the speed of the current. Some parties tack on an extra day at the beginning of the trip to spend time in town buying food, packing vehicles, and so on. Before making your sojourn into the wild, you'll need to do the following:

- Assemble a group of paddlers
- Consult guidebooks for details about the possible trips you have in mind
- Pick a suitable route based on season, access points, and so forth
- Gather additional information from local boaters or outfitters
- Call government agencies to find out whether permits are required
- Acquire any river or camping permits and fishing licenses you may need
- Check additional government regulations
- Arrange and plan shuttles
- Plan the menu
- Check the basic gear list
- Check the safety and rescue gear list
- Check the camping and cooking gear list
- Buy or rent any missing items or gear
- Check water levels or tides

- Check the weather forecast
- Check the difficulty of the journey
- Make certain that portions of the trip are not too dangerous to paddle

It's an intimidating list at first glance, but most paddlers actually find that plotting and then anticipating the journey is half the fun.

Fortunately, a wealth of information exists. Guidebooks have been published on hundreds of paddling destinations throughout the world. Some of these books concentrate on specific spots, and others describe a number of trips within a geographic region.

Topographic and nautical maps may also be useful to show the surrounding land features and potential places to camp. Some government agencies can provide camping information about the areas they manage. Maps designed for paddlers usually have campsite suggestions.

Don't forget public libraries. Many now have an interlibrary loan system through which you can request almost any book or map published. Other sources of information include members of boating clubs or knowledgeable employees at kayak shops. Now there's even the Internet, with web sites and bulletin boards dedicated specifically to kayak touring.

GUIDEBOOKS: KAYAK TOURING

There are a number of guidebooks written specifically for coastal touring by kayak. Some of the more noteworthy are as follows:

Sea Kayaking Canada's West Coast by John Ince and Heidi Kottner (Seattle: Mountaineers Books, 1992)

Sea Kayaking in Baja by Andromeda Romano-Lax (Berkeley, CA: Wilderness Press, 1993)

Sea Kayaking in Florida by David Gluckman (Sarasota, FL: Pineapple Press, 1995)

Sea Kayaking in the Florida Keys by Bruce Wachob (Sarasota, FL: Pineapple Press, 1997)

Sea Kayaking the Carolinas by James Bannon and Morrison Giffen (Asheville, NC: Out There Publishers, 1997)

Sea Kayaking the Mid-Atlantic Coast by Tamsin Venn (Boston: Appalachian Mountain Club Books, 1994)

Sea Kayaking the New England Coast by Tamsin Venn (Boston: Appalachian Mountain Club Books, 1991)

Kayaking Puget Sound, San Juan and Gulf Islands by Randel Washburne (Seattle: Mountaineers Books, 1990)

NAUTICAL CHARTS

Marine navigation's peculiarities make it somewhat more complex than terrestrial route finding. Beginners will no doubt be perplexed by the symbols and conventions used on marine maps, called nautical charts. The ability to read nautical charts and to relate them to features in the surroundings is essential to knowing where you are and avoiding potential hazards.

Nautical charts are published by the National Ocean Service (NOS), a division of the U.S. National Oceanic and Atmospheric Administration (NOAA), and by the Canadian Hydrographic Service. They can be ordered from these agencies or purchased from marine outlets.

Small-scale charts are those that cover a large area with minimal detail. For example, on a 1:250,000 scale chart, a foot on the chart equals 250,000 feet on the ground. Large-scale charts cover a smaller area but offer more detail. The 1:40,000 scale is a useful size for kayakers looking for detail.

The need for detail depends on the nature of the shorelines you will be paddling. If there are numerous offshore islands or complex channels, a large-scale chart (perhaps 1:40,000) is much better for staying oriented. A smaller scale such as 1:80,000 or 1:100,000 is adequate where coastlines are straight and offshore features are either few in number or large in size.

SOURCES OF NAUTICAL CHARTS AND MAPS

National Ocean Services
Distribution Division (N/CG33)
Riverdale, MD 20737

Eastern Distribution Branch
U.S. Geological Survey
604 South Pickett St.
Alexandria, VA 22304

Western Distribution Branch
U.S. Geological Survey
Box 25286
Federal Center
Denver, CO 80225

Canada Map Office
Surveys and Mapping Branch
Department of Energy, Mines,
and Resources
Ottawa, K1A 0E9
Canada

Captain's Nautical Supply
1914 4th Ave.
Seattle, WA 98101
(800) 448-2278

GREAT RIVER OUTFITTERS

Coastal navigation is an acquired skill.

TIDAL CURRENT TABLES AND CHARTS

Although tidal currents can certainly be dangerous, knowing about them is usually a matter of efficiency: It is far easier and faster to travel with a favorable current. Interestingly, tides themselves may be poor indicators of currents. The timing and the strength of tidal currents are predicted with annual tables designed for that purpose. In the United States, the NOAA publishes tidal current tables in a volume for the Pacific coast and another for the Atlantic and Gulf coasts, available from International Marine, P.O. Box 182607, Columbus, OH 43218, (800) 262-4729. In Canada, tidal current schedules are published in regional volumes by the Canadian Hydrographic Service.

Tidal current tables have two important parts. The first is a set of daily predictions for tidal currents in certain major waterways. The second part determines currents at other local places, using time and speed corrections applied to the daily predictions for the major waterways in the first part. Tide tables and tidal current tables are a necessity when you're paddling in areas affected by tides and you need to know the velocities of ebb and flow currents, information on rotary currents, and the movement of the Gulf Stream.

Although tidal current tables are the most precise resource for predicting currents at any time, they are tedious to use, especially in complex waterways where you are trying to see the overall picture of current flows in order to plan a route. Often the information in tidal current tables is extracted and applied to a current chart, making route planning much easier. Tidal current charts present a much more vivid picture of current flows, using arrows and correction factors to calculate speeds based on either tide tables or current tables. Tidal current charts are published by both the NOAA and the Canadian Hydrographic Services for such places as Puget Sound, the San Juan and Gulf Islands, San Francisco Bay, Chesapeake Bay, New York Harbor, Long Island Sound, and others.

The ability to read tidal currents is crucial for coastal kayakers.

GREAT RIVER OUTFITTERS

RIVER CONDITIONS

The amount of water flowing down a river is typically measured in cubic feet or cubic meters per second. This information is collected by various government agencies, and good guidebooks indicate which levels are best for paddling.

Information on river levels is readily accessible. Many newspapers publish flows of nearby rivers, and hot lines with recorded messages about river flow are available. For phone numbers or flow information, check with kayak shops and government agencies managing the river. If the river lies below a dam, call the agency managing the dam and ask about releases. Information can sometimes be obtained from state offices of the U.S. Geological Survey and the National Weather Service.

Hydrographs showing the flow each month for an average year are sometimes available from governmental sources. These are especially useful to kayakers in their long-term planning.

TRIP COSTS

Trip expenses may be fairly simple for small groups, or they may become complicated when a twelve-member group embarks on a two-week trip into a remote wilderness. For efficiency, groups usually pool their money. Before proceeding too far in the planning, it's best to make a cost estimate:

- How many vehicles will be used? What's the distance from your home to the destination and back? What's the distance involved in the shuttle? From this total mileage, you can estimate your gas costs.
- If you use the services of a commercial shuttle driver, add that expense.
- Based on the number of people in the group, estimate the cost of food for the trip.
- Add any expenses of renting equipment.
- Estimate costs of group supplies, such as stove fuel, batteries, and so forth.

With all this in mind, figure up the total and then add a margin of error. Always ask for more than you need. At the end of a trip, it's easy to refund money, but if you spend more than you have, it's sometimes unpleasant to collect it.

It may be a good idea to ask for a deposit early in the planning process. This will give you an idea of how many people are going. When people put their money down, it makes their commitment more serious.

GROUP DYNAMICS

A paddling group can range from one friend to a dozen or more companions. Smaller groups involve fewer planning hassles, and in many cases, there's less damage to the environment. In some areas managed by government agencies, you may be required to keep the party within a certain size. Some areas have become so popular that the number of boaters is causing environmental problems: Vegetation is trampled, campfire scars abound, and disposal of human waste presents sanitation problems. To minimize this impact, some government agencies have developed regulations to protect the natural resources, including systems whereby you have to apply in advance to obtain a permit to run the river or camp along the lake. Often a lottery is held. You have to write in advance—six months to a year isn't too early for the most popular sites. Information about permits is found in most guidebooks and sourcebooks.

For longer trips, the number of people planning to go will no doubt change. Changes in vacation schedules, illness, and a host of other circumstances can alter the list. You therefore need to make your plans flexible enough to adjust for a different-sized group. And regardless of the size of the group, everyone should be sufficiently experienced to handle the trip you're about to undertake.

GROUP PLANNING SESSIONS

Get your party together far in advance of the trip. Talk over dates, equipment, costs, and so on. Delegate duties, and put someone in charge of renting or borrowing additional boats and assembling other group gear. Then have a final group meeting a week, or just a few days, before the departure date. With a meeting that close to the departure, you'll have a better idea of exactly how many people are going. At this meeting, you can divide the responsibilities for last-minute details.

Food. Planning menus, buying food, and preparing meals can be done in several ways:

- All group members bring their own food and do their own cooking. This works best with small parties, when one stove or fire can be shared as each person cooks his or her own meal. With larger groups, food is typically bought collectively.
- One or more members of the group can volunteer to do all the menu planning, food buying, and cooking.
- The responsibilities for meals can be divided among the party. Each person is responsible for preparing a specific meal or meals for the group.

Collecting money. At the final meeting, collect the rest of the money. Some of it can be given to those buying food, and the rest can be used for gas, assuming equipment rental has been taken care of.

Personal equipment. Go over a list of personal gear, and be sure that everyone has adequate equipment and clothing for the trip.

Overnight trips involve careful advance planning.

GREAT RIVER OUTFITTERS

Expectations and safety. From the beginning, it's important that everyone knows that he or she is expected to help. The kitchen needs to be set up, boats loaded and unloaded, campsites pitched, and so on. If everyone is prepared to pitch in, the trip runs more smoothly, and there's more leisure time. Everyone should also realize that there are potential dangers in any wilderness travel. From a legal standpoint, as well as a moral one, make it clear that the trip will not be free from danger. After a review of the hazards, stress the importance of safety.

Environment. Remind everyone of the appropriate techniques to minimize environmental impact (explained in detail in chapter 9). Remember to use only biodegradable soap and to dispose of garbage properly. Consider the use of firepans to prevent damage to campsites. These and other precautions will help maintain our waterways in a pristine condition.

LEADERSHIP

There can be a designated leader on a trip, but more often than not, a democratic system develops. In certain situations in which the group has to make important safety decisions, inexperienced boaters should defer to opinions of the more experienced. As long as everyone maintains an easygoing attitude, things will proceed smoothly.

SAFETY IN NUMBERS

Traveling with an experienced group is no doubt the safest situation. On difficult trips, it may be better to organize a party of at least four or five boats so you have extra people to help if you run into problems. It's especially important to adhere to this rule when you're a beginner.

TRANSPORTATION

If you're planning a lightweight trip, transporting equipment may not present much of a problem. For longer trips, getting to and from the water can be more complex:

- Cartop racks can be used to carry kayaks on even the smallest of cars; a sturdy rack can be used for other gear as well.
- Pickup trucks, vans, and other sport utility vehicles are useful, but be careful not to load them beyond their recommended limits.
- Trailers can be rented or borrowed and are especially helpful for transporting a large number of kayaks.

On trips where vehicles are subjected to much wear and tear, you might consider reimbursing the vehicles' owners. It may also be a good idea to caravan in case car trouble develops. One last thing: Be sure that everyone knows exactly where you're going.

CARTOP CARRIERS

With the sophisticated line of car racks available, even the smallest sub-compact can transport several kayaks. The accessories for these racks are impressive, and you'll no doubt find the setup that fits your needs perfectly.

One option that is available with most racks is a set of saddles that conform to the curve of the boat's hull; this makes for a good fit and is less likely to deform a plastic kayak. Another option is called a kayak stacker. It is a vertically upright post fastened to the crossbar. It allows you to stack several kayaks on edge, thereby increasing the capacity of the rack.

Whatever car rack you use, make sure that the boats and gear are securely attached to the rack before you hit the highway. Most boaters use either heavy-duty elastic cord or nylon straps with strong metal buckles. Even more important, the bow and the stern of the boat should be securely fastened to the vehicle's bumpers. Specially made tensioners and hooks are available for this purpose, but the most foolproof system is a line that actually ties to the bumper.

SHUTTLES

Most kayak trips start at one point and end at another, so somehow you must shuttle your vehicles from one place to the other. The easiest solution is to hire a commercial shuttle driver. You can do your own shuttles by leaving one or more vehicles at one end and the others at the other end. This works well if there's not too much distance involved and you have plenty of time. Shuttles can involve an infinite variety of combinations, but the most common are these:

- Drive to the take-out and leave one vehicle there. Then, in the other vehicle, everyone drives to the put-in.
- Drive to the put-in and unload all the people and gear. Then drive the vehicles to the take-out. Leave all but one of the vehicles at the take-out and return all the drivers to the put-in.

Either way, you'll have to retrieve the vehicle at the put-in after the trip is over.

When performing a shuttle, make sure that the others know where you've put your car keys. Some people bring along two sets and keep them in separate boats in case of an upset. Others hide the keys on the vehicle itself so that the keys and vehicle are always together (be sure to hide the keys well). Also, be sure that you don't accidentally leave the keys to the take-out vehicle in the put-in vehicle.

One last note about shuttles and driving: Many consider driving to be the most dangerous part of a kayak trip, because vehicles are heavily loaded, drivers are sleepy, and everyone is anxious to get on the water. Whenever you drive, use care and caution.

PACKING THE KAYAK

Efficient packing begins with a checklist (see the sample at the end of chapter 2). After several trips, you'll no doubt develop your own. Carefully going through such a list is the only way to make certain that nothing is forgotten or left behind. A trip can be ruined if someone shows up at the put-in without a life jacket, or if everyone arrives in camp to discover that no one remembered to bring matches.

How gear fits into the kayak depends on the individual boat and the preferences of the person loading it. A number of waterproof bags made just for the small crevices of a kayak are available. Many kayakers carry a smaller "day bag" where they stow clothing and other items they'll want before getting to camp—camera, sunglasses, suntan lotion, gloves, lunch, and so forth. Keep a water container handy, too.

When you pack the kayak for the first time, or if you're trying a different load, test it at home to make sure everything fits. It's frustrating to arrive at the put-in and discover either that half your gear won't fit or that something you left behind would have fit after all.

To properly rig a kayak with camping gear, keep the heavy items low and toward the middle of the boat. The load should also be balanced as evenly as possible on both sides of the boat. Before you head out, take a short test run. If it doesn't feel right, paddle back to shore, rearrange it, and try again. Have another paddler check the water line of your boat. Before you hit the water, you'll want everything to be in order.

PART II

TECHNIQUE

5

GETTING STARTED

It's a beautiful sight: a double-bladed paddle dipping up and down, in and out of the water, like a bird's wings, to steer the kayak along a jagged coastline or across a wide expanse of lake. Behind these graceful motions is a kayaker working hard with the tool of his trade. Almost anyone with average strength and coordination can become proficient in the basic paddle strokes after a few hours of practice. Beginning on flatwater is best, because it's easier. To gain confidence, start on a small lake or in a swimming pool. Then you can gradually take your newly acquired paddling skills to a larger lake, a slow river, or a more challenging coastline.

Acquiring paddling skills is a matter of practice.

OLD TOWN CANOE COMPANY

THE BASICS

Before you start paddling, there are a few prerequisites that need to be tended to: things like entering and exiting the kayak, securing the spray skirt, emptying the kayak of water, transporting the kayak, and so on. None of these are particularly difficult—just unique to the sport of kayaking. With these preliminary matters behind you, it will be time to start focusing on your paddling strokes.

FINAL ADJUSTMENTS

Before you put the kayak in the water, you'll want to make sure that the foot braces are in the correct position. You should be able to brace both feet firmly against the foot braces while pressing your knees against the inside of the kayak, but you should also be able to relax and straighten your legs. This adjustment is worth getting right. If the foot braces are too close, your legs will soon become uncomfortable and grow numb. If the foot braces are too far forward, you will not have full control.

Step into the spray skirt and pull it up to just below the top of your chest, then roll the back inward so you don't end up sitting on it. Put on your PFD. You're now ready to enter the kayak.

Before setting out, a few adjustments are often needed.

ENTERING THE KAYAK

To enter the kayak without capsizing, you need to avoid putting all your weight on one side. To keep your center of gravity low, use your paddle as a steadying outrigger against the bank.

With the kayak in ankle-deep water, place the end of the paddle shaft across the rear of the coaming, and hold it in place with your fingers inside the coaming and your thumb around the shaft. With the opposite hand behind you, grip the shaft on the side you are entering. Now set one foot into the cockpit, and sit on the back deck, being careful not to put too much strain on the paddle. Place your other leg into the cockpit and slide down inside the boat.

SECURING THE SPRAY SKIRT

The best way to secure the spray skirt is to begin by fitting the hem of the skirt around the rear of the coaming. Next, put the front of the skirt in place. Then you can finish up with its sides. The spray skirt should fit tightly enough to keep water out, but not so tightly that it's difficult to release if necessary.

EXITING THE KAYAK

To exit the boat, you first need to remove the spray skirt. Then draw both knees toward your chest. Place the paddle behind you and—while holding it—grip the rear of the coaming with one hand. Grip the paddle shaft with your other hand to provide stability as the paddle blade rests on the shore. Carefully lift your foot out of the boat and place it on shore. Then do the same with your other foot. Now you can stand up.

CARRYING THE KAYAK

Smaller kayaks carried by one person are best carried on the shoulder. To get your kayak there, try this: Lift the boat by the front of the cockpit, and then place your shoulder into the cockpit, with the stern of the boat still resting on the ground. Then lean forward slightly to balance the kayak evenly on your shoulder. To pick up your paddle without bending over, try a quick flick of the foot to bring the paddle into your hand.

Larger sea kayaks, because of their bulk, are better carried by two people—one on each end—or with a kayak cart if only one person is available (or if the kayak is heavily laden).

EMPTYING THE KAYAK

Even with a good spray skirt, some water will inevitably enter the kayak. A small puddle is easy enough to remove with a sponge. For more than that, you can use a bilge pump, or on shore, you can have two people turn the boat over and then rock it up and down to remove the water. If you do this alone, prop one end on the ground, preferably against an object to keep it from slipping, and then perform the same rocking motion.

PADDLING STROKES

Paddling strokes can be divided into three major groups: power strokes, turning strokes, and bracing strokes.
- Power strokes propel the kayak forward or backward.
- Turning (or corrective) strokes move the kayak in a new direction or bring the kayak back on course.
- Bracing strokes provide stability, although some of them can also be used to turn the boat.

It's best to first learn and then practice the strokes in their pure form. With a little experience, you can then combine power and turning strokes into one smooth motion. This chapter concentrates on the basic power strokes—the forward stroke and the back stroke—which are not difficult but are important to get right. The next chapter discusses the turning strokes—the sweep and the draw—which are amazingly effective in turning the boat. Also covered are the bracing strokes—the low brace and the high brace—which are useful in wind and currents.

NANTAHALA OUTDOOR CENTER

It has been called "the Harvard of paddling schools" by *Esquire* magazine, and almost everyone in the paddling world knows (at least by reputation) the NOC near Wesser, North Carolina, and Great Smoky Mountain National Park. Founded in the early 1970s in an old motel and gas station on the banks of the Nantahala River, NOC is now a bustling community of kayaking instruction with an interesting range of guided trips, both at home and abroad. Contact Nantahala Outdoor Center, 13077 Hwy. 19 West, Bryson City, NC 28713, (704) 488-6737.

HOLDING THE PADDLE

Proper placement of the hands on the kayak paddle is crucial. The general rule for hand positioning is this: With the paddle set horizontally on top of your head, your forearms should form a 90-degree angle with your upper arms. Power and control will be lost if your hands are too close together, and the effective reach of the paddle will be reduced if your hands are too far apart.

Each hand should also be the same distance from the blades. This allows you to execute strokes with the same amount of power on each side.

Proper hand placement on the paddle is necessary for controlling the boat.

If your hand placement is uneven on the shaft, one side will naturally have more leverage than the other. As a result, the boat will tend to turn to the opposite side—a common, but frustrating, experience for novices.

MOVING THE PADDLE

The blades of most kayak paddles are feathered, and adjustment of the blade is necessary, depending on which side of the boat you are stroking. Each hand has a different job in making the adjustment. The majority of feathered blades are spooned in such a way as to require what is known as either right-hand control or left-hand control. Right-hand-control paddles are by far the most common.

The grip of the control hand on the shaft (in this case, the right hand) never changes during paddling, but the wrist of the control hand does flex. The other hand—the noncontrol, or slip, hand—loosens to allow the shaft to rotate back and forth through the stroke. Therefore, as you make a stroke on the right side with a right-hand-control paddle, you rotate the

It is best to learn and practice strokes on flatwater.

shaft with your right hand so that the blade enters the water in the correct position. Simultaneously, your left hand relaxes a bit to allow the shaft to rotate.

To stroke on your left side, rotate the shaft with your right hand so that the left blade enters the water properly. Then grip the shaft firmly with your left hand as you pull the left blade through the water. The turning of the shaft with each stroke ensures that the blade just removed from the water slices neatly through the air, offering little or no wind resistance.

If your paddle is left-hand-control, your left hand turns the shaft while your right hand relaxes.

Beginning paddlers sometimes rotate the shaft partially with both hands. This causes blade distortion, because the control hand is

A good paddling stroke aims for smoothness and efficiency.

compromised. Rotating the shaft with both hands also makes it difficult to perform precise strokes. An oval shaft helps somewhat with this inadvertent twisting.

The other problem for novice paddlers is that the noncontrol hand tends to travel toward the middle of the shaft. This offsets the power delivered to each blade and causes the kayak to veer.

FORWARD STROKE

The forward stroke is the standard power stroke. Because it's instinctive, many paddlers think that it requires little discussion: Just place the paddle in the water and pull. However, there is much more to this stroke than meets the eye, and proper form can make a huge difference—not only in performance but also in how tired you are at the end of the day.

The forward stroke is basically a cycling movement of the arms and shoulders. It is similar in principle to pedaling a bicycle, and to be efficient, it must be executed with precision and smoothness. The key to the forward stroke is to use the heavier muscles of the torso rather than the arms alone.

Setup. The setup is the foundation of a good forward stroke. First, extend your paddling arm forward by rotating your shoulders, torso, and abdomen. If you flex the same-side knee up, it will help rotate your hip forward. This, in turn, helps twist your torso and shoulders into the correct setup position. When you extend the paddle by twisting your torso, you're arranging your body to allow the powerful muscles of the back and abdomen to be unleashed during the power phase. The hand of the extended arm needs to be over the boat's midline, and remember to remain upright. Tempting as it may be, *don't* bend at the waist to get a good forward reach.

KAYAK SYMPOSIUMS

During the year, sea kayakers come together at symposiums and workshops to exchange ideas. Listed below are a number of the better-known ones. For more information, contact Trade Association of Sea Kayaking (TASK), Box 84144, Seattle, WA 98124, (206) 621-1018.

- Advanced Coastal Kayaking Workshop. Contact: L. L. Bean, Inc., Freeport, ME 04033
- Alaska Pacific University Kayak Symposium. Contact: Alaska Pacific University, 4101 University Dr., Anchorage, AK 99508
- Angel Island Festival & Regatta. Contact: Sea Trek Ocean Kayaking Center, Liberty Ship Way, Sausalito, CA 94965
- Atlantic Coast Sea Kayaking Symposium. Contact: L. L. Bean, Inc., Freeport, ME 04033
- East Coast Sea Kayaking Symposium (Charleston, SC). Contact: TASK, Box 84144, Seattle, WA 98124
- Great Lakes Kayak Touring Symposium. Contact: Great River Outfitters, 3721 Shallow Brook, Bloomfield Hills, MI 48013
- Hornby Island Kayaker's Festival. Contact: Hornby Paddling Partners, RR 1, Hornby Island, British Columbia, V0R 1Z0, Canada
- Inland Sea Kayaking Symposium. Contact: Trek & Trail, Box 906, Bayfield, WI 54814
- Jersey Shore Sea Kayaking & Bay Canoeing Show. Contact: Ocean County Dept. of Parks, Lakewood, NJ 08701
- Mystic Sea Kayaking Symposium. Contact: Mystic Valley Sikes, 26 Williams Ave., Mystic, CT 06355
- West Coast Sea Kayaking Symposium. Contact: TASK, Box 84144, Seattle, WA 98124
- West Michigan Coastal Kayaking Symposium. Contact: Lumbertown Canoe & Kayak Specialties, 1822 Oake Ave., North Muskegon, MI 49445

A fluid, even stroke is the result of attention to detail.

Catch. The catch is the point where the paddle enters the water. A good catch is critical for maximum power and efficiency, because it places the blade in the vertical position necessary for effective application of power. A good, solid catch gives the blade a firm grip on the water so that the boat moves forward in relation to the stationary blade. A combination of downward movement with the pulling arm and forward thrust with the pushing arm immerses the blade. Strive for a splashless catch: If your paddle blade enters the water cleanly, you don't waste energy, and the blade has the correct vertical orientation.

Power. Now you apply power to the paddle. If you're performing the forward stroke correctly, most of the power comes from the untwisting of your torso. The pull from the lower arm also contributes to the force of the stroke (the push from the upper arm contributes the least). The lower arm pulls backward until the hand is near the hip. Bringing the paddle back any farther wastes time and power. At this point, both arms are relaxed, with the upper arm dropping down.

Recovery. This action causes the blade to rise to the surface of the water, so that the stroke can begin again. The trick is the timing. If you take out too early, you cheat yourself of some power. If you take out too late, the blade drags and slows the boat. To exit at the correct time, start pulling the blade out of the water when your lower hand becomes even with your hip. Try to avoid lifting up water. To do this, take the blade out of the water by pulling it out to the side, away from the boat. Now the setup position can begin for another stroke. To keep the boat moving smoothly, make a quick transition to the next stroke before the boat starts to slow down. Avoid an uneven stop-and-go movement.

In executing the forward stroke, only a slight rotation of the body and shoulders should accompany the arm motion. Eliminating unnecessary body motion allows for greater smoothness and efficiency. Use the stronger and larger muscles of your back, abdomen, and upper body. Uncoil your body, keep your arms straight, and make your shoulder and stomach muscles do the work.

Having an experienced boater watch you execute the stroke can be very helpful in improving your form. So can watching that same person perform the stroke. A number of good videos are also available on paddling technique.

STERN RUDDER

Even if you have a good forward stroke, there's still the problem of veering. Apply power to the right, and the kayak turns to the left, and vice versa. To keep the boat going in a straight line, the paddler must use some sort of correction stroke. It is better to apply small correction strokes before the boat veers too much. But when the boat has veered substantially, it's necessary to apply a more powerful correction stroke.

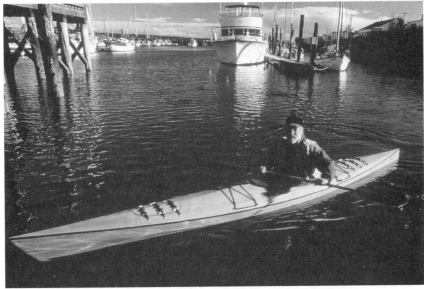

PYGMY BOATS, INC.

Small corrective strokes prevent the kayak from veering.

The most abrupt correction stroke is a stern rudder, in which the paddle is held along the side of the boat to bring the boat back on course. This rudder stroke is very effective, but it also creates excessive drag and therefore slows the boat's forward speed.

BACK STROKE

The back stroke is basically the reverse of the forward stroke. The main difference is that you don't insert the blade as far from your body as you do with a forward stroke. As a result, it's a much weaker stroke.

To start the stroke, dip the paddle into the water slightly behind you. The back side of the blade (the nonpower side in a forward stroke) is now the power side, even on a spooned blade. Lean back a little, instead of bending forward at the waist. The bottom arm pushes down and forward, while the upper arm pulls up and back. This stroke uses the muscles of the abdomen, arms, and shoulders, and it's necessary to keep a steady, erect posture. Remember, too, to keep the paddle vertical and close to the boat.

A more extreme form of back stroke occurs when you rotate your shoulders and head around so far that you are almost facing backward. You can twist your wrists to dig the power face of the paddle blade into the water near the stern and pull it toward you as your body slowly uncoils. When the blade reaches your hip, you return the blade back to its proper forward position and continue to push it forward.

6

ADVANCED STROKES

Once you've mastered the basic power strokes, you're ready to learn the turning strokes—the sweep and the draw. You'll be amazed at how quickly the kayak responds to one of these strokes, when properly executed. After you've perfected the turning strokes, you'll want to practice the static support strokes, called bracing strokes, especially the low brace and the high brace. When you've mastered all these, you're on your way to becoming a proficient kayaker.

PIVOT POINT

The point around which the boat turns is called the pivot point. It is usually close to the center of the boat, but the pivot point can change, often dramatically. One important factor affecting the pivot point is the distribution of weight in the boat. When the paddler shifts his or her weight to one side of the boat, as in an eddy turn, the pivot point naturally shifts. Another factor is the accumulation of external forces. For example, when

Turning strokes, properly executed, move the boat quickly.

KAYAKING VIDEOS

There are a number of excellent how-to videos for touring kayakers:
- *Performance Sea Kayaking: The Basics and Beyond*
- *Sea Kayaking* (Trailside Series)
- *Over and Out* (sea kayaking rescue)
- *Greenland Style Kayaking*

These videos can be obtained from Great River Outfitters, 3721 Shallow Brook, Bloomfield Hills, MI 48302, (810) 683-4770.

the boat initially accelerates, the pivot point moves toward the stern, but when the boat moves forward under constant power, the pivot point moves toward the bow.

The pivot point is important to turning strokes. A sweep stroke, for example, taken near the pivot point has little effect. Take that same sweep stroke farther toward the end of the boat—away from the pivot point—and the boat responds immediately.

LEANING THE BOAT

Intentionally leaning the kayak is an important aspect of paddling skill. Leans can keep you from flipping over and are commonly used when turning and bracing. The key is to lean your boat, not your body. This point cannot be overemphasized.

The best way to lean the boat is to lift up with the knee of one leg and push down on the seat with the other leg. At first this will make you feel unstable, but with practice, you will be able to hold the boat on edge for some time.

As you lean the boat, you have to bend sideways at the waist to maintain your center of gravity. You will be sitting upright relative to the water, but you will be tilted in relation to the boat. Keep your body over the midline of the boat, not over to either side.

SWEEP STROKE

When executing turns, kayakers can make good use of the sweep stroke. In sweep strokes, you use the same basic technique as for regular forward and back strokes, except that the sweep is an exaggerated arc out and away from the boat. Because it turns the boat quickly, the sweep is also useful in shallow water and meandering creeks.

GREAT RIVER OUTFITTERS

Mastering the strokes allows a paddler to negotiate challenging waves.

You want the paddle to be as far from the pivot point as possible in order to increase the leverage of the stroke. It's this extra reach that gives the stroke more power. To get the most from the sweep, use the muscles of your torso as well as your arms.

FORWARD SWEEP

The forward sweep, like a forward stroke, pushes the bow away from your paddling side—but much more dramatically. Best of all, you lose no forward momentum with this stroke. Thus, a forward sweep on the right moves the kayak to the left. A forward sweep on the left moves the kayak to the right.

To execute a full forward sweep, make the stroke as far as possible from the center of the boat. Plant the blade and rotate your torso, spinning the boat in a circle. Body rotation is essential to an effective sweep stroke. While making the stroke, keep your arms straight and the paddle blade well away from the boat. Finish with the paddle behind you and almost touching the stern. It is permissible to lean slightly forward or back, but try to maintain good posture during the stroke. It is also possible to make a half forward sweep by simply stopping the stroke halfway through the arc.

Make sure that you put your abdominal, shoulder, and back muscles into the sweep. The sweep will be compromised if it is performed with the arms alone. While you sweep, lift up your corresponding knee to gain additional power.

Remember, too, that the boat will turn more sharply when leaned to the outside. So if you lean slightly to the side of your sweep, you'll produce a faster turn. But don't lean too much, or the boat will stall.

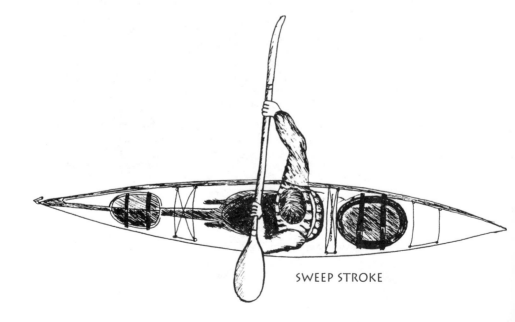

SWEEP STROKE

REVERSE SWEEP

The reverse sweep is completed the same way as the forward sweep, except that the paddle blade starts at the stern of the boat and ends at the bow. The reverse sweep pushes the stern toward your paddling side, much like a back stroke, but more dramatically. Thus, a reverse sweep on the right moves the kayak to the right. A reverse sweep on the left moves the kayak to the left.

Start the reverse sweep with your paddle as far back and as close to the stern as possible. Push the water in an arc using the back face of the paddle blade. The most effective part of the reverse sweep is the beginning of the stroke, so give power to the stroke early.

Avoid the common mistake of confusing a reverse sweep with a back stroke. The half reverse sweep, starting at the stern and ending at a right angle to the boat, is a common correction stroke on whitewater. Unfortunately, instead of a reverse sweep, many paddlers place the paddle behind them and push forward, making a back stroke. This kills the speed of the boat.

BRITISH CANOE UNION INSTRUCTION

The premier British paddling association is the British Canoe Union (BCU), which sets safety standards and offers instruction. The BCU now offers sea kayaking courses in the United States through the following companies:

Atlantic Kayak Tours
320 W. Saugerties Rd. 7
Saugerties, NY 12477
(914) 246-2187

Great River Outfitters
4180 Elizabeth Lake Rd.
Waterford, MI 48302
(810) 683-4770

Maine Island Kayak Company
70 Luther St.
Peaks Island, ME 04108
(800) 796-2373

Sweetwater Kayaks
5263 Ocean Blvd., Siesta Key
Sarasota, FL 34242
(941) 346-1179

Trek & Trail
P.O. Box 906
222 Rittenhouse Ave.
Batfield, MI 54814
(800) 354-8735

DRAW STROKE

Another useful turning stroke is the draw stroke. The draw stroke quickly moves the boat sideways toward the paddle. Thus, a draw stroke on the right moves the kayak to the right. A draw stroke on the left moves the kayak to the left. There are variations, the bow draw and the stern draw being the most common.

Start the draw by reaching out with a vertical paddle and plant the blade with its power face facing you. Extend your top hand as far out as possible to maintain a vertical paddle. Pull (or "draw") the paddle toward the kayak. Just before the paddle reaches the kayak, turn your hand away from the kayak. If you want to execute another draw stroke, move the paddle blade back to the catch position.

Twisting your torso so that you face the paddle helps with the draw stroke. Lift up with your corresponding knee to keep the boat level. Otherwise, the boat will have a tendency to lean into the direction of the draw, which can destabilize you.

Try not to let the paddle hit the side of the boat. If you let the paddle go under the boat with any speed, it can act like a fulcrum and flip you over.

Paddling strokes depend more on the torso than the arms.

PYGMY BOATS, INC.

BRACING STROKES

Experienced kayakers can make good use of bracing strokes, which utilize the paddle as a lever to provide stability. There are two basic forms of braces: a low brace and a high brace. With a brace, you're actually using the force of the water to keep the boat upright. It's important to remember that on a river you must always lean and brace downstream. Leaning upstream will almost always cause you to capsize.

LOW BRACE
The low brace is useful when the kayak suddenly tips toward your paddling side. The low brace feels as if you're pushing off the water to stabilize yourself. To use a low brace, reach out with a nearly horizontal paddle, so that both hands are away from the boat. Using the back face of

LOW BRACE

HIGH BRACE

the paddle, apply a quick downward push on the surface of the water. As you push against the water, lift up with the knee that's on the side you're flipping toward. At the same time, snap your hips, which helps bring the boat upright. The combination of hand placement over the water and the thrust of the paddle moves the boat back to a stable, upright position.

HIGH BRACE

The high brace is useful when the kayak suddenly tips away from your paddling side. The high brace feels as if you're grabbing the water with the power face of the paddle to pull yourself upright. It is much like a draw stroke, though it's stationary and executed quickly.

One precaution is in order for the high brace: Avoid allowing your wrists to move too far behind and above your head. In powerful water, this position invites the possibility of a dislocated shoulder.

THE WET EXIT

Even if you're paddling gentle waters, it's a good idea to be prepared for the possibility of turning over. Many beginning paddlers think that they'll be trapped in the boat if this happens. Their fears are completely groundless. Getting out of an overturned kayak is easy—you simply fall out of the boat.

To understand what happens, place your hands on the sides of the boat, take a deep breath, and then slowly turn the boat over by leaning to one side. When you're upside down, remove your knees from the knee braces and draw your feet up. As you do this, pull the spray skirt off the cockpit by the loop attached to the front of it. When you relax, you will automatically slip out of the cockpit. You can then push the boat away with your feet.

Practice the wet exit with a paddle, and try to hold on to the paddle. With your paddle and the boat's grab loop in one hand, use the other hand to propel yourself to shore.

Whenever you exit your boat, always maintain contact with it. The easiest way to do this is to keep one hand on the cockpit's coaming as you come to the surface of the water. Then you can swim quickly to the bow or stern grab loop. It's best to keep the kayak upside down when towing it to shore after a wet exit. It will ride higher in the water because of the air trapped inside.

THE ESKIMO ROLL

The Eskimo roll—the complete overturning of the kayak followed by a self-recovery full circle to an upright position—is one of the most dramatic maneuvers in kayaking. Surprisingly, it's a skill that anyone can learn with

LARRY WORKMAN/DAGGER CANOE CO.

Practicing strokes on a calm lake allows you to concentrate on form.

PADDLERS' TALES

This report comes from Joanne Turner on paddling the coast of Hong Kong:

"With much anticipation, I assembled my folding kayak on the beach at dawn in about thirty minutes. Its nylon-rubber skin stretched tightly over a frame of aluminum-titanium, setting up much like the backpacking tent it would carry for the week's trip. I checked my compass bearing and compared it with the chart in a plastic cover on my deck and with the profile of the islands visible in the distance. Paddle in hand, I headed southwest from Pui-O on the island of Lantau in the New Territories of Hong Kong.

"My boat was secure and seaworthy. The weather was warm and clear, with a small 1-foot swell coming toward me. But these waters were different. The smells and sights and sounds challenged my senses and thoughts. I passed a coconut painted with a Chinese character used as a float for fishing nets, floating in the waters among the islands, and a handmade horsehair brush used for painting cloth and wood throughout much of Southeast Asia. But most curious were the fishing families aboard the junks and trawlers, most all of whom motored over to see what kind of tiny red craft was moving through their waters. I was as foreign in their waters as finding a coconut float was unusual to me."

a little work. Many touring kayakers never learn the skill because they paddle gentle waters, and even those who learn it find the Eskimo roll unreliable unless they practice it often.

Imagine trying to describe in words how to ride a bicycle or climb a ladder. It's not only difficult to do, but difficult to comprehend. Very few people have learned how to Eskimo-roll by just reading about it, which is why most kayaking how-to books don't attempt to describe it in detail.

To learn a new skill like the Eskimo roll, it's far better to watch someone actually perform it. Doing so in person is obviously the best way, and watching a videotape is second best. If at all possible, seek the assistance of an instructor or an experienced paddler to help you learn this skill. He or she will be able to spot what you are doing wrong and provide helpful suggestions. In the process, you'll learn the roll much more quickly. A pair of goggles to watch someone else perform the roll is invaluable, and a pair of nose clips will make the experience more comfortable when it's your turn. A helmet and life jacket will only get in the way at this point, so don't worry about them until you've learned to roll first.

As with most skills, there is more than one way to do the Eskimo roll, but most rolls are basically the same. The key to any roll is the hip snap. Although it takes the entire body to accomplish the roll, it is really the action of the hips that rotates the boat upright. One common mistake made by beginners is raising the body above the water before doing the hip snap, which is too soon. The upper body move should follow the hip snap.

It's also helpful to realize that the roll is really nothing more than a sweeping brace done underwater. In brief, the roll works like this: When you're upside down in the water, you must crouch your body close to the surface of the water and at the same time place the paddle in position on the surface of the water for the sweep stroke that will follow. You then sweep the paddle out from the boat in a wide arc. The angle of the blade as it moves through the water is critical. A climbing angle will keep the blade high in the water and near the surface. Then you execute the hip snap, which is a combined motion of the hips and knees to flip the boat upright. Your body, however, remains in the water. The last step in the roll is a high brace, which lifts your body out of the water after the boat has been flipped upright.

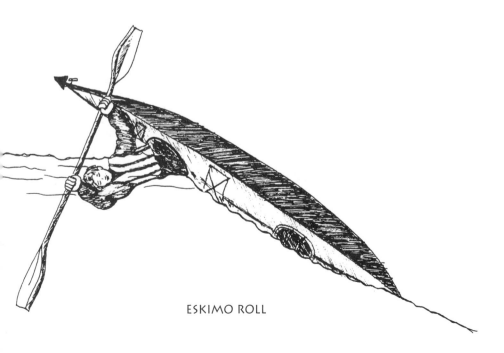

ESKIMO ROLL

SEA KAYAKING SKILLS

Serious sea kayaking involves not only good paddling skills but also that difficult-to-define concept known as "water sense." Water sense is a blend of training and common sense that creates an experienced and competent paddler who can make well-informed decisions and handle emergencies. Among other things, it includes the following:

• Ability to "read" water
• Balance and "feel" of the boat on the water
• Technical paddling skills
• Understanding of critical elements such as weather and tides
• Carefully honed instinct

In sea kayaking, water sense might mean, for example, recognizing how kelp beds indicate the direction and strength of tidal current, predicting how big the waves will be halfway out on a 2-mile crossing, or sensing when a big storm is on the way.

There are a number of excellent books to help you with these sea kayaking skills, such as *Derek C. Hutchinson's Guide to Expedition Kayaking on Sea and Open Water* (3rd ed.; Old Saybrook, CT: Globe Pequot Press, 1995) and *The Complete Book of Sea Kayaking* (4th ed.; Old Saybrook, CT: Globe Pequot Press, 1994). Also highly recommended is *Nigel Foster's Sea Kayaking* (Old Saybrook, CT: Globe Pequot Press, 1997).

7

WIND, WAVES, AND CURRENTS

They call it "reading" water—that special skill that boaters have of evaluating a stretch of water to determine which route and which technique will provide the least chance of damage to gear and to themselves. Reading water is more of an art than a science, and as with all fine arts, there is more than one way to do it well. With that said, there are still a few basic principles that allow boaters to better size up those intimidating currents ahead.

As a beginning boater, you should hone your skills first on lakes and other flatwater. Then you can try your hand at slow-moving water that offers little in the way of obstacles. After you're comfortable with that, you can gradually move to slightly more difficult water. That way, you'll never find yourself in a situation you can't handle. Experience may be the best instructor, but you should try to develop your technique in controlled conditions and take advantage of opportunities to paddle with more experienced people to see how they handle waves.

WIND AND WAVES

Wind and the resulting waves can be just as much a hazard on a lake or along a coastline as rocks and rapids are on a river. The following techniques will help you deal with these problems.

HEADWINDS

The techniques for paddling into headwinds are important to keep the kayak from capsizing. Before crossing open waters, study your map or the horizon for a route that offers the best wind protection and the most possibilities for getting off the water should the wind increase. To hold a kayak on course while heading into the wind, you need to paddle hard with quick and effective correction strokes.

Dealing with wind and waves is kayaking's greatest challenge.

As waves increase in size and speed, the top of the wave curls over in a dangerous condition known as a breaking wave. As the breaking wave approaches, try to turn the bow straight into it. You'll lose some forward speed, but pushing straight into the waves reduces your chance of capsizing. When whitecaps occur, it is time to get off the water.

Headwinds are generally the least threatening winds, although big waves may get you wet because the bow doesn't have time to lift over the rapidly oncoming waves, particularly if the boat is heavy with gear. These waves are not likely to cause a capsize, because you are more likely to punch through big waves rather than be surfed backward.

Paddling into wind is always drudgery. Progress is slow, and the paddling effort may strain the arms. If you carry a spare paddle that is shorter or has a narrower blade, it may help. Try for a steady cadence with long strokes, head forward for more reach, and less body profile in the wind. Try to time the strokes just ahead of the waves to help the bow lift over them. In gusts, give yourself a rest, and then try to progress each time the gusts subside.

Quartering into headwinds—attacking them at an angle—may be the best tactic. In heavy breaking waves, however, the waves should be taken head-on. Attack the waves and always lean *into* them, never away. When quartering into waves, try to time your strokes to help you climb over the wave. This helps the boat accelerate down the back side of the wave.

The ability to read water is essential.

CROSSWINDS

Paddling crosswinds requires another set of tactics. Even in a light crosswind, you may be blown sideways, and as a result, you will arrive downwind of your desired destination. As crosswinds increase, the risk of being rolled over by the waves also increases. To avoid these problems, you need to angle into the waves, known as quartering the waves. Remember to turn the bow into large breaking waves to avoid capsizing. Then lean into the wind and waves. Leaning into the wind balances the wind's force and reduces your wind profile slightly.

In strong crosswinds, the wind also tends to lift the blades on a feathered paddle. To reduce this problem, you can use a narrow-bladed or unfeathered paddle, or you can try to keep the blades as low as possible or avoid strokes during gusts.

WEATHER WATCHING

For the serious sea kayaker, the new interactive computer program for recognizing and dealing with bad weather at sea is highly recommended. It is entitled *Starpath Weather Trainer*, by David Burch, and is available from International Marine, P.O. Box 182607, Columbus, OH 43218, (800) 262-4729.

The major factor in crosswind paddling is the tendency to capsize on the downwind side. Therefore it's best to lean toward the wave as it approaches. In more rounded waves, a slight lean is sufficient, but in steeper waves and stronger winds, more lean is needed.

When you see an especially large, breaking side wave coming, you can brace into the wave and take it sideways; if you do so, the brace must be sustained until the wave loses its grip on you. Or you can turn into it and punch through it. If you see a particularly big wave coming, you can often use an intervening wave crest by turning when the center of the boat is on the crest and the boat is easy to spin around.

TAILWINDS

You may think that paddling tailwaves is simple because the wind is behind you. This may be true in light winds, but as wind and waves increase, tailwinds can become challenging. Running downwind is the least comfortable direction of travel and is the worst way to be going when winds get really bad. One problem is that you can't pay attention to what is happening behind you.

When the wave comes from behind you, it pushes the stern up, and the kayak starts to pick up speed as it surfs down the face of the wave and buries its bow in the wave ahead. As the wave passes under the kayak, it may pivot the boat sideways into the trough created between the two waves. If this happens, you can easily capsize. To keep the kayak from turning into the trough, you must use a strong rudder or draw stroke.

Although downwind paddling is faster, it can be stressful because of the constant acceleration and deceleration associated with each wave's passage. But the most persistent problem is the boat's tendency to turn sideways, known as broaching, across bigger waves. The faster you go, the greater your directional instability and vulnerability to broaching forces. Once a broach starts, there is little that can be done to correct it, and you'll end up sideways to the wave, where capsize is likely.

On smaller waves, the broaching tendency is less severe, and you may be able to head it off with well-placed sweep strokes or rudder strokes. The rudder itself may also be used to correct the boat's tendency to veer off course. Slowing down, particularly on the front of waves when you tend to surf ahead, may help. If none of this works, lean forward and brace.

Regardless of your precautions, traveling downwind in conditions that produce unavoidable broaches is nerve-racking and slow. Sometimes it's best to look for another way to get to your destination or wait the storm out.

Wind has its advantages.

COASTAL WINDS

Mountainous coastlines tend toward strong winds, and very strong gusts are possible in inlets on the lee (downwind) side of mountains as air is pushed over the peaks and then dropped rapidly on the other side. In warm climates, a sea breeze is likely on sunny days. As the land heats during the day, warmed air rises, creating a low-pressure area and drawing cooler marine air in to fill it. These onshore winds typically develop in late morning or early afternoon and continue until a few hours before sunset. As a result, mornings are usually the calmest times of day, unless some other weather system moves in and exerts its own influence. Paddling open water or places of exposure should therefore be done as early as possible or at the end of the day.

TIDES AND TIDAL CURRENTS

The timing and the strength of tidal currents are predicted with annual tables and charts designed for that purpose (see chapter 4). Although the strength of a current is related to the size of the tides, topography of the waterway is most important. Strong currents are most likely where the tide falls between two adjacent bodies of water unevenly, producing a difference in water levels and a powerful flow. The flow direction of a tidal current depends on whether the tide is flooding or ebbing, and the current's strength or speed is related to the ongoing tidal exchange.

In their most severe form, strong currents can produce abrupt differences in the direction of flow such as whirlpools, boils, and other heavy hydraulics, which challenge even the most competent paddler. In such places, the kayaker should schedule his or her paddling for the period of least activity, when the currents slow and turn to the other direction.

The biggest problems occur when the wind and the current oppose each other. With even a moderate wind, a tide change bringing an opposing current can cause bigger waves with shorter intervals that are more likely to break. How bad the waves will become depends on current speed, wind strength, and the length of open water over which waves can build.

Tide rips are patches of closely spaced and sometimes breaking waves. Most tide rips are little cause for concern if you have developed reasonably good paddling skills and a sense of balance in your boat. Others produce waves that any kayaker would want to avoid. The best tactic with tide rips is to keep a sharp eye out ahead and go around ones that look too challenging.

Tidal currents can present real hazards to boaters.

PADDLERS' TALES

This report comes from Colin Lilley on paddling the coastline of northern Spain:

"As we paddled clear of the Cabos the swell remained a considerable size and there was always the risk of a rogue breaker. Then there was a horrendous surf sweeping against Salinas beach. We cruised just outside the breakline. Was it safe to go in? We decided eventually that it was breaking too far offshore and that it was just too big, so we paddled into the nearby Aviles harbor and found a rough campsite near its mouth. At last we landed after five hours of continuously paddling seas that were the most exhilarating we had experienced. Our feelings were a mixture of satisfaction and relief. Gazing back out, the sea appeared calm. The large expanse of the Bay of Biscay, the blue skies, the warm sun, and the inviting beaches belie the real power of the sea."

If you find yourself unable to avoid being pulled through a tide rip, stop trying to get away and head into it. Keep up a fast and short paddling cadence in the rip so that each stroke can be turned into a small high brace, to counter whatever the irregular waves do to your balance. Remember that the current will likely carry you out the other side if you can pay attention to keeping your stability.

BASIC NAVIGATION

When you find yourself in a situation that requires you to constantly refer to a nautical chart to pinpoint your location, it's important to place the chart in an easily accessible and visible place on the boat. This is especially true when you're in unfamiliar and complex terrain. To make the chart manageable, it's usually best to fold it or cut out the appropriate pages. The chart can be inserted into a plastic bag or, better yet, a chart case with a zip closure or roll-down seal. The case can then be placed under the deck lines just ahead of the cockpit for easy reference. Your intended course, tidal current times and strengths, and other information needed to paddle a particular route can be included in the case.

Navigation is a subject to which entire books have been devoted. The following is a brief review of basic navigation.

GREAT RIVER OUTFITTERS

Marine navigation is a subject to which entire books have been devoted.

NAVIGATION BY GPS

Because a global positioning system (GPS) can automatically and effort-lessly pinpoint your position anywhere in the world within about a hun-dred yards, many boaters are using it to relieve the tedium of a compass and nautical chart. Like all electronic devices, though, it can fail, so a com-pass should be carried as a backup.

NAVIGATION BY REFERENCE POINTS

Navigating by reference to topographic features around you, such as a shoreline, is one of the most common methods, but it can be more difficult than it seems. The key is to always stay oriented to your location on the chart in front of you. In most places, where shorelines are fairly linear and islands are not too numerous, it's easy, but where there's a maze of islands and channels, losing track, even momentarily, can quickly lead to dis-orientation.

Whenever you come around a point of land and a new vista opens up ahead, immediately try to identify all the newly visible features on your chart. To head out in one direction on a false assumption about surround-ing landforms may cost you untold time and frustration.

NAVIGATION USING A COMPASS

Steering with a marine compass mounted on the kayak deck is easy. You simply keep the desired course number centered over the mark that faces toward you. Without visual cues for orientation, steering with a compass takes a little getting used to, but with a little practice, you will develop the right response to bring yourself back on course. A hiker's compass can also be used, but it is more complex. Highly recommended is the book *Be Expert with Map and Compass* by Bjorn Kellstrom (New York: Collier Books, 1994).

NAVIGATION BY DEAD RECKONING

Dead reckoning is following a compass course for a specified time and speed. For example, if you need to paddle through still water to an island 4 miles to the south, a dead-reckoned course steered south at 4 miles an hour should get you there in one hour. This technique is most often used to reach destinations you cannot see from your departure point and when there are no fixed reference points along the way.

Dead reckoning still requires a large amount of guesswork. It's difficult to know exactly how fast you are paddling, and it's difficult to steer exactly in a straight line. Then there are the elements of wind and current, which are usually present to throw off your calculations. Trying to reach a small, isolated island by dead reckoning is difficult, but it may be a practical method for crossings when the landfall is too big to miss.

Those who use topographic maps are familiar with the headaches of declination—the difference between true and magnetic north. Fortunately,

---

FINDING YOUR WAY

The premier reference for navigational matters is *Fundamentals of Kayak Navigation* (2nd ed.) by David Burch (Old Saybrook, CT: Globe Pequot Press, 1993). No serious sea kayaker should be without it. Here are some other excellent navigation books you should have:

The Essential Wilderness Navigator by David Seidman (Camden, ME: International Marine, 1995)

Boat Navigation for the Rest of Us: Finding Your Way by Eye and Electronics by Bill Brogdon (Camden, ME: International Marine, 1995)

Celestial Navigation for Yachtsmen (rev. ed.) by Mary Blewitt, edited by Thomas C. Bergel (Camden, ME: International Marine, 1996)

Emergency Navigation: Pathfinding Techniques for the Inquisitive and Prudent Mariner by David Burch (Camden, ME: International Marine, 1989)

The Practical Pilot: Coastal Navigation by Eye, Intuition, and Common Sense by Leonard Eyges (Camden, ME: International Marine, 1989)

most marine charts have a compass rose, which is a red or purple numbered circle that allows you to find what compass course you have to steer to get from one place to another on the chart. The inner ring of numbers on the compass rose shows magnetic bearings, and the outer ring shows true bearings. As long as you use the inner ring, no corrections from the chart to the compass are needed.

You can estimate the paddling time to your destination by dividing distance in nautical miles measured on the chart by your speed in knots. If there is a significant current flowing perpendicular to your course, you have to adjust your course to compensate for the distance you are carried with the current. Keep in mind that speed estimates derived from current references are based on one point in a channel, and currents elsewhere may produce a different overall speed than predicted. Wind-caused drift is a more difficult factor to anticipate. If the wind is strong enough to require a dead-reckoning course adjustment, do not attempt the passage unless the destination is large.

FORECASTING MARINE WEATHER

Although some radio and television stations include marine weather forecasts, the best sources are the continuous VHF broadcasts provided by the National Oceanic and Atmospheric Administration (NOAA) in the United States and the Coast Guard in Canada. You can receive these broadcasts in most coastal regions and many large inland waters of North America. You can use a multiband radio with a weather band or a small, inexpensive weather radio that tunes only to these frequencies. Handheld marine VHF transceivers pick up all weather frequencies and often receive them clearly when other radios cannot.

Marine forecasts covering the next twenty-four hours focus on wind speed and direction and the size of waves for various areas. They also include visibility limits because of fog or drizzle and, for the outer coast, swell size and direction. A small-craft advisory is issued if winds are expected to rage. This forecast is a good reason to stay on the beach unless you are willing to challenge your good paddling skills or unless your route is well protected from the predicted wind direction. Never go out on the water if gale warnings or storm warnings have been issued.

For a long trip in an unfamiliar area, knowing about the weather patterns or likely weather conditions (whether to expect headwinds or tailwinds, for example) in the area for the month of your visit can help you plan your distances. A book called *U.S. Coast Pilots*, published by the National Ocean Service, has good weather summaries and tables of weather statistics by month. Elements of interest include wind direction, expressed as a percentage of days having winds from each sector and days of no wind, and the average strength associated with each direction. Many areas have a direction from which the strongest winds blow, usually associated with bad weather.

RIVER CURRENTS

Much can be learned about how a river works by simple observation. Spend time studying moving water and how it is affected by the obstacles it encounters. The key to running a river is an understanding of the river—its currents, form, and flow.

BENDS
A river's tendency to meander causes erosion of its banks. As this erosion continues, the current gradually carves out a new bend, and the current begins to pile up on the outside of the bend. The inside of the bend becomes increasingly shallow.

The deepest and fastest current is usually found along the outside of the bend. This current naturally has a tendency to move the boat to the outside of the bend—which, unfortunately, often contains large boulders, overhanging trees, undercut cliffs, and other hazards.

EDDIES
Currents called eddies generally move upstream, either behind rocks or behind projections along the bank. The slack water on the inside of a bend is also referred to as an eddy, even though it doesn't move upstream.

The imaginary line between the main current and the eddy is known as the eddy line, where the currents between the eddy and the main current mix and swirl. Currents along the eddy line can be very powerful, even capable of moving the boat back upstream.

Eddies are useful for boaters entering or leaving shore, and they can be used to stop the boat in midstream. Some eddies, especially those of the swirling, whirlpool variety, should be avoided because they are capable of trapping a boat and rotating it indefinitely.

ROCK RECOGNITION
Huge boulders peeking above the surface of the water are obvious. Low-lying rocks are more problematic. Those hidden boulders just below the surface of the water are sometimes called sleepers. Watch for the characteristics that signal them: Water piles up on the upstream side of a rock,

creating a pillow, which may or may not cover the rock entirely. Look, too, for the rooster tails shooting up above or behind a rock.

A series of waves tends to be regular in configuration, and rocks below the surface tend to upset the pattern. If the last wave in a series doesn't fit the pattern, a rock may be lurking underneath. Look closely, too, into the white froth for a glimpse of darkness that signals a rock.

PILLOWS

When the river's current collides with a rock, some of it forms an upstream mound called a pillow. As the mound grows in size, it eventually spills over, creating a hydraulic. When the pillow deflects spray into the air, it's called a rooster tail.

Pillows should usually be avoided, because they may conceal an undercut rock or ledge, allowing the current to dive underneath. These are especially dangerous because they can entrap a swimmer.

REVERSALS

Rocks protruding above the surface of the river are easy to spot. But when water flows over the top of a rock and into the slack water behind it, the water creates a backflow as it moves upstream and then back on itself.

Reversals come in various shapes and sizes. Knowing the difference between friendly and not-so-friendly holes is the boater's most important skill.

Small holes present little trouble. But there are holes that can stop a boat—appropriately called stoppers.

How do you determine when a wave is a reversal? When a rock is just underwater, it may be difficult to spot from upstream because there's little turbulence. Try to look for a calm spot in the midst of turbulence. Usually the rock deflects the current, and as a result, the water levels out as it sweeps over the rock. Viewing a reversal from shore often allows you to see rocks that aren't visible from the river. Other rocks are concealed by spray and can be seen only with steady concentration.

STANDING WAVES

When fast currents are followed by slow ones, the water starts to pile up. If the transition is gradual, there is turbulence in the form of standing waves. These are sometimes called wave trains or, if they're at the end of a rapid, tailwaves. When standing waves converge, they surge randomly in a phenomenon called haystacks.

If the wave is high but gradual, it's best to approach it bow-first, allowing the boat to ride over the crest. If the waves are steep and angular, and there's a chance of overturning, it's normally a good idea to move to the side, where the wave is usually more gradual than at the center.

First, however, it is best to make sure that the waves are in fact standing waves. Rocks just below the surface can create mounds of water that only appear to be standing waves. Careful observation is required: Standing waves are regular and patterned, whereas waves concealing submerged rocks are usually more jumbled. These irregular waves, known as backcurlers, can overturn an unwary boater.

SWEEPERS AND STRAINERS

During spring floods, rivers can contain a lot of debris: fallen trees, branches, and logs wedged between rocks. River runners call these obstacles sweepers (downed trees that allow current to flow through but may trap a boat or swimmer) and strainers (where the river filters through boulders). The force of water moving into such obstacles can present an extremely dangerous situation.

A skilled kayaker must be able to deal with rocks and waves.

8

SAFETY MATTERS

Until you've actually been there, it's difficult to imagine the force of a wave pounding down on a boat out of control, or the danger of hypothermia if you overturn in cold water. Like most outdoor pursuits, kayaking can be dangerous, but most accidents can be prevented with a little foresight. A healthy attitude of caution is perhaps the best safety precaution of all.

According to expert Randel Washburne, there are four levels of defense for kayaking safety:

- Avoid trouble by understanding changeable weather conditions, currents, and tides.
- Survive rough seas by bracing, handling strong waves, and avoiding a broach.
- Recover from a capsize using the paddle float and other recovery and reentry techniques.
- Signal for help with flares, strobes, or radios.

The failure of any one of these levels of defense brings into play the skills associated with the next level, and weakness in any one skill burdens the rest. The first levels are the most effective, and the fewer levels you need, the better your chances of survival. For example, assuming proficient skills, preventing a capsize in rough seas is always easier than recovering from one in the same conditions.

PERSONAL PREPARATION

The best safety measures are preventive. Sharpening paddling skills, staying in good physical condition, keeping equipment in good repair, and researching the territory you plan to cover are all important. Still, accidents do happen, even to the most experienced paddler, and being prepared just makes sense.

It's always a good idea to start on easy water early in the season and gain some experience before moving on to more difficult water. When

GREAT RIVER OUTFITTERS

The best safety measures are preventative.

paddling into an area you're not familiar with, collect everything you can: guidebooks, maps, magazine articles, and reports from other boaters.

On the water, try to maintain a fairly relaxed pace, and be sure to allow plenty of time for negotiating hazards or dealing with unexpected wind conditions. It's also important to know the proper procedures for rescuing boaters and boats. Remember, too, that most accidents don't happen on the water—they happen in camp. The consequences of your actions are certainly made more serious by remoteness from the city.

Those who lead trips have special responsibilities. They must collect maps, guidebooks, and detailed information about the trip. They must also be aware of changes in weather or water conditions and how these will affect the trip. They should review with the other boaters safety and rescue matters, and leaders must also check the gear: life jackets, first-aid kit, repair materials, and survival equipment. They must give their plans to the appropriate authorities in case rescue is needed, and they must determine points of assistance in case of emergency.

ADEQUATE CLOTHING

The advice for clothing is fairly straightforward: Always wear adequate clothing to protect against cold water and sunburn. The biggest threat presented by cold weather and water is hypothermia, the condition in which the body loses heat faster than it can be generated. It can result in death if the heat loss isn't stopped. If you dump in very cold water, you must get out immediately, even if this means abandoning your boat to swim for shore. Even with protective clothing, hypothermia can set in quickly (see the detailed discussion on hypothermia later in this chapter).

EQUIPMENT PRECAUTIONS

Making sure that your boat is in working order is very important, especially on remote trips. You should also make certain that your safety equipment is adequate.

PFD. The most indispensable piece of safety equipment is the life jacket, or personal flotation device. It must provide sufficient flotation for the water you'll be tackling.

Rescue line. In rescue situations, plenty of rope is the key. For boat rescue, there should be at least 50 feet available. Carabiners will also come in handy.

First-aid kit. A good first-aid kit is imperative. Be sure that it's adequate for the duration and the remoteness of the trip you're taking, and that it's dry and well stocked with the following:

Assorted Band-Aids	Antibacterial ointment
Assorted bandages (Ace, triangular, etc.)	Scissors
Adhesive tape	Antihistamine cream
Gauze roll	Sun protection
Water purification tablets	Snakebite serum
Aspirin	Tweezers
Seasickness pills	Safety pins
Plastic tubing	Pain killer
Antiseptic cream	First-aid book

Repair kit. The repair kit should include not only repair materials for boats, but other equipment as well, such as paddles, rudders, and tents.

Helmet. In rocky areas where overturning is even a slight possibility, a helmet provides an important measure of safety. On easier waters, a helmet isn't necessary, but on more difficult waters, a helmet could save your life. As with life jackets, there are many models of kayaking helmets on the market. The best ones are designed somewhat like bicycle helmets and have a plastic shell completely lined with foam. Most models that cover your ears provide good protection. Although a snug fit is absolutely necessary for adequate protection, you can get a headache if your helmet is too tight. Some helmets are adjustable, but many come in various sizes. If your helmet is somewhat loose and nonadjustable, it's possible to glue foam inside it to tighten the fit.

Safety knife. Also helpful are safety knives. Most kayakers wear these knives upside down on their PFDs so the knives are readily accessible. A serrated edge is more efficient for cutting ropes, and a double-edged knife is better yet.

Bilge pump. Carry a good bailing device, and make sure that it's securely fastened to the boat.

Flotation bags. Some recreational kayaks are not designed to carry much gear, since the extra weight compromises maneuverability. Instead of bulkheads, these boats depend on

Helmets provide a measure of safety in rocky areas.

flotation bags—a short one in the bow in front of the foot braces, and a larger one stuffed in the stern directly behind the cockpit. For boats with foam pillars, there are half-sized bags that fit on either side. Even in touring kayaks with bulkheads, you may want to insert flotation bags for added safety. Unlike a canoe, a swamped kayak will sink if air isn't trapped inside. Proper flotation keeps a swamped boat riding high in the water.

Whistle. A whistle can be a useful safety device to communicate with other boaters at a distance.

Gloves. Blisters can ruin a trip, and a good pair of paddling gloves can help prevent them.

Emergency signaling devices. Flares, strobe lights, signal mirrors, VHF radios, and EPIRBs (emergency position-indicating radio beacons) may be necessary, depending on the circumstances.

GROUP TRAVEL

Never boat alone. Most boaters travel in groups of two or more for greater safety. The boat with the most experienced paddler leads the way, determining the best route and waiting below as the rest of the paddlers come through. Another experienced boater should run a "sweep" boat behind the group to make sure that everyone makes it through safely and no one is left behind.

BEEN THERE, DONE THAT

What more effective way to teach safety at sea than a collection of real-life scenarios by those who have gotten into trouble and lived to tell about it? It is entitled *Sea Kayaker's Deep Trouble: True Stories and Their Lessons from* Sea Kayaker *Magazine*, by Matt Boze and George Gronseth, edited by Christopher Cunningham (Camden, ME: Ragged Mountain Press, 1997).

Each boater should keep the one behind in sight at all times. This is especially true on a large body of water with windy conditions. Inexperienced boaters should never pass the lead boat.

Although staying close together, boaters should increase the distance between them while running dangerous, rock-studded waters. Crowding together not only restricts maneuverability but also increases the chance of collision, as well as the chance of forcing a boat against rocks or other obstacles. There should be sufficient distance between boats that if the first boater sees trouble, he or she can stop immediately. Group travel also works well for the rescue of swimmers and boats if an emergency should develop.

A set of hand or paddle signals, agreed on at the beginning of the trip, can be helpful in communicating from boat to boat. This is especially true where there is some distance between boats and communication is difficult. Signals should be simple—a paddle outstretched horizontally for "stop," a waved paddle for "help," and a paddle outstretched vertically for "all clear."

NIMBUS PADDLES

The boat with the most experienced paddler leads the way.

HYPOTHERMIA

Hypothermia is the lowering of the body's temperature to a dangerous level. Any boater exposed to cold weather—and especially cold water—can become a victim. Symptoms of hypothermia typically include fatigue, apathy, forgetfulness, and confusion. Shivering may or may not occur.

Once the body is thrust into cold water, the brain begins to conserve body heat by constricting blood vessels in the arms and legs. Shivering usually (but not always) begins as the body attempts to generate heat. Then the body's core temperature starts to drop. As it falls below 95 degrees, the person has difficulty speaking. Further decreases bring on muscle stiffness, irrational thinking, amnesia, and unconsciousness. When the core temperature falls below 78 degrees, death occurs. In near-freezing water, the time from immersion to death can be as short as ten minutes.

Awareness of the causes of hypothermia—and the speed with which death can occur—is the most important aspect of prevention. Treatment is simple, but the sooner it is begun, the better. First, replace wet clothes with dry ones, and move the person into a warm shelter. If the person is unable to generate his or her own body heat, rewarming is required. Hot liquids may help, but never give someone with hypothermia alcoholic drinks, which dilate blood vessels, allowing even greater heat loss. Heat from a supplemental source should also be provided. If it's impossible to build a fire, body heat from others (lightly clothed, for best results) is helpful. If the person becomes unconscious, the situation is extremely serious, and hospitalization is required as soon as possible.

Hypothermia can be prevented, to a large extent, by adequate clothing, proper food, and good physical conditioning. The best clothing for cold conditions is a wet suit or dry suit. The food you eat is also important: Sugar and carbohydrates are quickly oxidized to provide heat and energy. Physical conditioning can also be a factor, so it pays to stay in good shape.

SELF-RESCUE IN OPEN WATER

If you should capsize, the most important technique to know how to perform is a self-rescue. Even with other paddlers around, it's easier and faster for you to rescue yourself than to depend on someone else.

Most importantly, don't panic. Remember to hold on to your paddle, because you're going to need it once you're back in the boat. Next, look for your boat. In most cases, it will be right next to you. This is where handholds come into play. The bottom of the kayak is smooth and slippery and therefore difficult to hold. The grab loops at the bow and stern offer good handholds, as does the cockpit.

Using a paddle float. Self-rescue with a paddle float has been used successfully by many solo kayakers in rough water, and it is an important piece of equipment for anyone who paddles alone. Because no help can be expected, practicing this technique is critical.

The necessary elements are a float securely attached to the paddle blade and a means to fix the paddle firmly to the deck to stabilize the boat. Many sea kayaks are designed with a flat deck behind the cockpit and a pattern of bungees to secure the paddle.

PADDLE FLOAT SELF-RESCUE

RESCUE OF A BOATER IN OPEN WATER

The following recovery method works when a paddler has capsized and other paddlers, still in their boats, are there to assist. These procedures may appear straightforward and simple, but the movements will not come naturally in rough, cold water, so it's best to practice them.

This rescue technique requires only one rescuer, and it is usually effective unless the victim is extremely tired, weak, or hypothermic. The recovery begins by inverting and emptying the capsized kayak. Then the rescuer pulls alongside, with the victim on the far side of his or her own boat. The victim passes the paddle to the rescuer, who lays both paddles across the decks of the two boats. The rescuer's primary job is to steady the victim's kayak as he or she reboards, which is usually not too difficult unless the victim is much heavier than the rescuer or is clumsy with fatigue.

The grip on the victim's cockpit is the key. The two paddles should be positioned across both cockpits and trapped under the rescuer's forearms to aid stability. The rescuer pulls both boats tightly together and leans across to distribute his or her weight over the two kayaks. The victim can then pull his or her upper body onto the rear deck before crawling into the cockpit.

HYPOTHERMIA SYMPTOMS

99–96 degrees F. The body starts to shiver intensely and cannot be controlled. The victim cannot do complex tasks.

95–91 degrees F. The victim still shivers violently and has trouble speaking clearly.

90–86 degrees F. Shivering decreases or stops, and the victim cannot think clearly. The muscles are stiff, but the victim keeps his or her posture. Total amnesia may occur.

85–81 degrees F. The victim becomes irrational and drifts into stupor.

80–78 degrees F. The victim becomes unconscious and does not respond to the spoken word. The victim's heartbeat becomes irregular, and there are no reflexes.

Below 78 degrees F. Death occurs as a result of complications arising from failure of the cardiac and respiratory centers in the brain. These may include cardiac fibrillation and pulmonary edema. There is hemorrhage in the lungs.

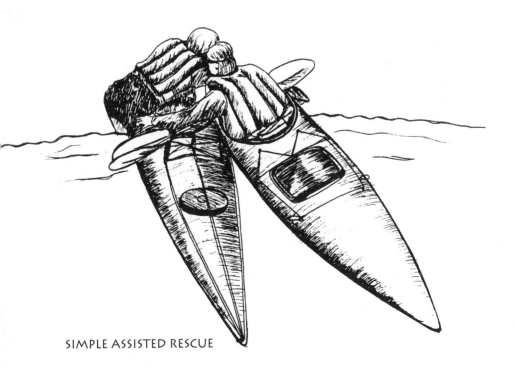

SIMPLE ASSISTED RESCUE

EMERGENCY SIGNALING DEVICES

The first lesson in rescue is to make your boat and person visible to search-and-rescue craft. First, stay with your boat. Kayaks are far easier to spot than swimmers. Boats and clothing in white, yellow, international orange, or neon colors are best for visibility in the water, especially in poor light. Reflective tape on paddle blades, deck, or PFD shoulders is especially effective.

There are numerous emergency signaling devices that you might carry, all with different effectiveness in varying situations. The key is having more than one type of backup on hand.

FLARES AND SMOKE DEVICES

Flares come in several types. Meteor flares use a rocket to propel the light hundreds of feet into the air and then burn while falling. Parachute flares do the same, except that the light burns much longer aloft, suspended under a little parachute. Handheld flares, which last about two minutes, are good locators but have limited visibility at a distance.

The most popular meteor flare for sea kayakers is a pencil-type flare called the Skyblazer. It is small and inexpensive, ascends to about 500 feet, and burns with a fairly bright light for six to eight seconds. But because these flares are brief, and because they can fail to ignite, you should carry at least six of them.

Parachute flares, though quite expensive, are major attention getters—often achieving twice the height and brightness of a meteor flare. Since parachute flares drift a considerable distance with the wind, they should be fired so that they drift over you.

Handheld flares should be held as high as possible to increase their visibility. However, the more popular ones drip hot residue, so hold the flare horizontally at its far end.

Flares are less effective in bright sunlight, in which case a smoke device is preferable. It emits a large cloud of bright orange smoke that is visible on sunny days, though the wind may dissipate the cloud and keep it low on the water, where it is hard to see. Smoke devices may be handheld or come in a canister that is ignited and tossed into the water. Both last about a minute.

STROBE LIGHTS

Strobe lights are probably the most effective nighttime signal, and they are also quite visible during the day. The main advantages are that they have a long life if the batteries are maintained, they are reliable (and testable, unlike flares), and they can be switched on or off, depending on whether a potential rescuer is visible.

SIGNAL MIRRORS

Though mirrors carry no official approval, search-and-rescue pilots think highly of them for locating victims in sunny weather, even from long distances. A signal mirror should be made of noncorrosive stainless steel and have a lanyard to prevent loss.

VHF RADIOS

Handheld radios are generally the most effective emergency signaling devices. Marine VHF radios (radios that use very high frequency channels dedicated to marine users) usually have a range of 5 to 10 miles and must be licensed with the Federal Communications Commission (FCC). Once the Coast Guard has received your call for help, its rescue helicopters can home in on your signal as long as you keep pushing the transmit button periodically.

Almost all marine VHF radios receive weather forecasts and local condition reports broadcast continuously by either the National Oceanic and Atmospheric Administration (NOAA) in the United States or the Canadian Coast Guard. These radios can pick up these channels in marginal conditions when cheaper weather radios will not. Marine VHF radios can also be used to make telephone calls to anywhere in the world via marine operators.

A few accessories are important for your VHF radio. Most important is a special plastic bag that will keep water off the radio and keep it afloat. A telescoping antenna can double the radio's range compared with a short, flexible rubber antenna.

EMERGENCY POSITION-INDICATING RADIO BEACONS

The Class B EPIRB sends a signal on aviation distress frequencies that can be picked up by a network of satellites anywhere in the world. The signal can pinpoint your position within 5 miles. (Class A is identical, except that it turns on automatically when immersed.) Class B EPIRBs are the most effective device when you are paddling in remote areas. Because signals are not investigated until confirmed by a second satellite pass or other evidence, they probably will not provide a quick enough response to save you if you are swimming in cold water.

The Class C EPIRB emits signals on marine VHF radio frequencies, so the range is only about 5 to 10 miles. Unfortunately, many boaters may not recognize distress calls from an EPIRB, and the likelihood of a response is uncertain. If someone does understand it, however, the response would be much quicker than to a Class B EPIRB.

Although EPIRBs cost several hundred dollars, they are reliable and attract attention from a huge radius. They are also waterproof and float. They must be licensed with the FCC.

PADDLERS' TALES

This report comes from Jim Ross on paddling Baranof Island:

"In the course of the following week we made our way north up the fjord-indented coastline of the west of Baranof Island. Several paddling days were lost due to depression after depression rolling in from the Pacific. On at least one occasion we had set out in favorable conditions, only to be overtaken by rapidly deteriorating weather an hour or so later, producing force-six to -seven winds and 30-foot swells with breaking waves. It was in advanced conditions such as these that the personal skills and abilities of the group were tested. Living in continuously wet conditions and paddling in difficult seas along an unforgiving coastline was perhaps the time to reflect that should an accident occur, we were practically beyond outside help. Group safety was paramount, and it was better to miss a day paddling than to risk being swept upon a rocky lee shore where an accident would result in the loss of a kayak.

"The possibility of reaching help overland, through thick rain forest or over snow-covered passes, was out of the question. Reliance could not be placed on summoning help with our VHF marine radio, which used line-of-sight transmission over distances not much over 10 kilometers, or on the personal locating beacon that we carried and that required a satellite overhead to pick up our signal. We were on our own.

"Finally, the weather broke and we were able to paddle among idyllic islands and to watch the wildlife around us. Sea otters, seals, and bald eagles had become common sights. Traveling by kayak enables one to approach seabird colonies silently, and even whales feel safe enough to come within 5 meters to look us over.

"During the previous wet, cold days, the vision of the hot springs at Goddard, a day's paddle short of Sitka, was sufficient incentive to keep spirits high. There can be nothing more luxurious than to peel off clothes caked with salt and wood smoke, climb into a tub overlooking the sea, and lie soaking up the warmth of the water and the beauty of the surrounding wooded islands and the dominating outline of Mount Edgecumbe, the extinct volcano on Kruzof Island."

PART III

CAMPING SKILLS

9

SELECTING CAMPSITES

It has been a long day of paddling, you're tired, and there's nothing like pulling into a warm, comfortable camp in the middle of a vast, unspoiled wilderness. Life is good, thanks to a fortunate choice of campsites.

WHERE TO CAMP

On some public lands, you may not have a choice of where to camp if the managing government agency assigns campsites. But in most areas, the choice of a campsite is up to you. If you're near private land, you should take into consideration the rights of landowners.

Most campers believe that a suitable campsite should have at least a good landing spot and a large flat area for tents. These are just the basic principles of campsite selection; many other considerations come into play.

Kayaking is an excellent escape from city life.

PYGMY BOATS, INC.

Natural protection. In bad weather or windy conditions, you'll want to find a more protected area surrounded by bushes or trees. Caves and rock overhangs may also be helpful in protecting you from the elements.

Shade. In hot weather, shade is an obvious attraction. In the desert, its availability is often limited, so keep a close eye out for it.

Breeze. If it's hot, a pleasant breeze may be welcome, so look for a more exposed area.

Mosquitoes. In areas where mosquitoes and other insects are a problem, beaches and gravel bars are preferable to heavily infested grassy and overgrown areas. A swampy area may usher in a horde of mosquitoes at twilight, and a soft, grassy spot may be full of chiggers.

Flood considerations. If you're located in an area prone to flash flooding, be sure that you have an escape route to higher ground.

Sandy beaches. Sandy beaches are clean and feel wonderful underfoot, but there is a downside: Eventually the sand finds its way into everything.

Drinking water. It's nice to have fresh drinkable water at your campsite, but don't count on it. Instead, fill your water containers at every opportunity. Be sure to boil or purify all drinking water.

Off-the-water activities. Keep an eye out for places to hike, or perhaps an interesting landmark to investigate.

Other attractions. If you have a choice of sites, you may want to consider whether it has a swimming hole, sunshine in the morning, a pile of driftwood for a fire, good fishing, and so forth.

Many factors are involved in finding the right camping spot.

Environmental considerations. Beach and gravel bar campsites are preferred because environmental damage can be kept to a minimum. Grassy areas, if heavily used, become trampled and gradually lose their vegetation as

OLD TOWN CANOE COMPANY

boaters pass back and forth. If it's necessary to sleep in a grassy or vegetated area, try to do the cooking on rocks or sand along the shore.

Gravel bars at first seem inhospitable places for erecting a tent and placing a sleeping bag. But the inconvenience is well worth getting away from bugs and having an open view. The biggest problem is finding a comfortable place to sleep, but that concern is alleviated with the thick foam or inflatable pads now available. Self-supporting tents also make it easier to pitch a camp in almost any location.

Life is good, thanks to an excellent choice of campsite.

OLD TOWN CANOE COMPANY

DOWN THE YELLOWSTONE

Steve Chapple, burned out from living too long in the big city, moved back to his native Montana, took a few kayaking lessons, and then, with his wife and two sons, paddled the length of the Yellowstone River—at 671 miles, the longest free-flowing river in the lower forty-eight states. The adventure, including colorful descriptions of the interesting personalities he met along the way, is chronicled in *Kayaking the Full Moon* (New York: HarperCollins, 1993).

BOOKS ON KAYAK CAMPING

These two books are recommended for those who have to stuff camping equipment and food into the confines of a kayak:

Kayak Camping by David Harrison (New York: Hearst Marine Books, 1995)

Kayak Cookery by Linda Daniel (Birmingham, AL: Menasha Ridge Press, 1997)

THE ROUTINE

While some of the group set up tents, others can get the stove or fire going and the cooking under way. When planning a trip, one decision is whether to use a stove or build fires. Where there's little driftwood and the area has been scoured for wood, stoves are a must. Where driftwood is plentiful, a fire may be acceptable if certain precautions, such as using a firepan, are taken. To ensure an evening's supply, pick up driftwood before reaching camp.

A number of other housekeeping chores also need to be taken care of, such as unpacking the kitchen and setting up the latrine. All these activities have environmental consequences, which are covered in detail in the next section.

TRACELESS CAMPING

Kayakers tend to be protective of the paths they paddle, which is fortunate for those of us who follow. It may be that kayakers are more likely to appreciate the natural world they're escaping to, or less likely to spoil the beauty that took so much effort to reach. Whatever the reason, it's important to tread lightly on a resource that can be loved to death—and unintentionally destroyed in the process.

GARBAGE

In the total scheme of things, what difference does one candy bar wrapper thrown to the wind make? The answer is a lot, especially when the single effect is multiplied, as it invariably is.

The rule for disposal of garbage is simple: Carry it all out. The best method for doing so is a plastic garbage bag placed inside a more resilient

NIMBUS PADDLES

It's important to tread lightly on a resource that can be loved to death.

nylon bag. Keep a small bag handy for use during the day, and be careful to collect even the smallest piece of paper.

If you're using a campfire or charcoal briquettes, burn all trash possible, but remember that aluminum foil packets will not burn, and certain foods, such as eggshells, require more time than a short morning fire. If the garbage can't be burned, dispose of it by placing everything except liquids in the garbage bag (grease, in particular, should always be carried out).

Liquid garbage, such as coffee, soup, and dishwater (containing biodegradable soap), should be strained first. The solids remaining can then be thrown into the garbage bag. In wooded areas, which foster rapid decomposition, the liquid can be poured into a single hole dug for that purpose, at least a hundred feet from any area normally used for camping. In wooded areas that are heavily used, it may be better to pour the liquids into the main current of the river, where they will quickly disperse—but first check with the government agency managing the river. In desert regions, which don't foster rapid decomposition, the liquid should be poured into the main current or in the middle of the lake, rather than at the shore.

One way to avoid garbage in the first place is to plan ahead: Select foods and packaging that will result in as little trash as possible.

THE CAMPFIRE

For many kayakers, staring into the flames of a campfire is the ideal way to end a day of paddling. But in some areas, fires have left scars that will take decades or more to heal, and trees have been stripped of their branches, and even cut down to provide firewood. Even collecting deadwood can damage the environment if not enough is left to replenish the soil with nutrients and to provide shelter for birds and animals.

One solution is to ban campfires and to use only stoves for cooking. Doing so would certainly eliminate the need to light fires, but it would also take some of the pleasure out of wilderness travel. Most ecology experts agree that a complete ban on campfires isn't necessary. It's important, however, to treat fires as a luxury and to ensure that they have the smallest impact possible.

Fires may have to be banned, for example, when dry conditions render the fire risk high. In some areas, fire permits may be required, and you may have to carry a stove. Such regulations seem restrictive, but they prevent further degradation. Fires, officially permitted or not, are inappropriate in some areas anyway. In particular, fires shouldn't be lit near and above the timberline because of the slow growth rate of trees and the soil's need to be replenished by nutrients from deadwood.

In other areas, fires can be lit even on pristine sites without significant harm to the environment, as long as you take certain precautions. You should leave no sign of your fire: Do not leave behind partially burned wood. Refill the shallow pit you've created with sod or with the dirt removed when it was dug; spreading dirt and loose vegetation over the site helps conceal it. The ideal place for fires is below the flood level along rivers, since any traces will eventually be washed away.

Do not build a ring of rocks around a fire—the campsite soon becomes littered with blackened rocks. Although the idea is to contain a fire, the best way to do so is to clear the area of flammable materials; a radius of a couple of feet is large enough. You should also make sure that there are no low branches or tree roots above or below the fire. Pitch your tent and other gear well away, preferably upwind, so sparks can't harm it.

If you camp at a well-used site with many rock-ringed fireplaces, use an existing one rather than making a new one. Take time to dismantle the other fire rings, removing any ashes and charcoal as garbage. Some designated backcountry sites provide metal fireboxes that, when present, should be used.

If you collect wood, do so with care. First and foremost, do not remove wood—even deadwood—from living trees; this is needed by wildlife and adds to the site's attractiveness. Nothing is worse than a campsite surrounded by trees stripped of their lower branches and a ground bare of any fallen wood. In high-use areas, search for wood farther afield. Collect only what you need, and use small sticks that can be broken by hand, which are easily burned to ash.

Build the fire where it will have less impact: either below the high-water mark on a rocky shoreline or in a bare spot where it's easy to remove all remains. Build as small a fire as you can. An entire meal can be cooked with amazingly little wood. When you're finished with the fire, thoroughly douse it with water, and restore the site to its former condition. Throw any blackened rocks into the water.

DISHWATER

The best method for disposing of dishwater is to dig a small hole, carefully removing any sod. Use this same hole for all dishwater while at the campsite; the soil elements will rapidly cause it to decompose. The hole should be situated away from the camp and above the high-water mark. When you're ready to leave, fill in the hole, pack down the soil, and replace the sod so that it's indistinguishable.

Never dispose of dishwater, leftover food, or soap in side streams or the main river unless you're in the desert or unless you're advised to do so by the government agency managing the river. On a few rivers, such as the Colorado, there's less environmental impact if the dishwater is first strained of any solid food particles or coffee grounds (which are packed out as garbage) and then disposed of in the main current (not the eddies) rather than on land. Use this procedure, however, only on rivers where it is specifically recommended.

HUMAN WASTE

To reduce the impact of human waste disposal, bury the waste (after carefully burning the toilet paper) in a hole about 6 inches deep—the best depth for soil elements that cause rapid decomposition. Carry a small backpacker's trowel, and make the hole at least 100 feet from the river's high-water line and away from any area normally used for camping.

10

THE KITCHEN

Among kayakers, cooking styles vary. Some boaters prefer lavish, four-course meals with fresh fruits and vegetables, and others like the lean and easy-to-prepare backpacker fare of dehydrated and freeze-dried foods. How you intend to eat largely determines the type and amount of cooking gear you'll need. With either extreme, modern technology has made the job easier.

GENERAL CONSIDERATIONS

Cookware typically consists of the standard set of aluminum or stainless-steel nesting pots, which are lightweight and compact. A cast-iron or Teflon-coated griddle and frying pan may come in handy for certain menus.

Many boaters still cook over an open fire, which is usually acceptable as long as certain precautions are taken (see chapter 9), but many kayaking cooks prefer the consistent heat of a white-gas or propane stove. The number of models has proliferated, and their sophistication and durability have gone a long way in making the cook's life an easier one.

Depending on the menu, you'll need other cooking utensils such as a can opener, serving fork, cooking spoon, serving spoon, carving knife, paring knife, potato peeler, turning spatula, tongs, and so on. A roll-up pouch with compartments makes for better organization of these utensils. Refillable polyethylene tubes, with removable clips on the end, are handy for storing butter and other spreadables. Also useful is a hard-plastic egg carton and a spice container with slots for half a dozen spices. Now there's even a miniature espresso maker for camp stoves. A necessity is a pair of pot-gripper pliers for handling hot cookware.

CAMP STOVES

Camp stoves offer a number of advantages: They reduce the need for campfires—and their resulting environmental impact—and they ensure that you have hot food and drink when you want it. At the end of a long day, when you're pitching camp and feeling tired, setting up a stove is easy. Gathering wood and building a fire take more time and effort. In foul weather, a stove enables you to cook hot meals in the warmth and shelter of your tent.

Differences in the makes and models of camp stoves are significant, but charts comparing the weights, fuel consumption, and boiling times of various stoves can be misleading. Many factors affecting a stove's performance in the field can't be duplicated in a controlled environment, and individual stoves of the same model can perform differently. In some situations, a malfunctioning stove is a nuisance. At other times, it poses a serious problem, particularly if lighting a campfire is impossible. Some stoves work well in the cold and wind; others don't. Waiting for a stove to produce hot water when you're wet and cold is annoying, but if you're on the verge of hypothermia, it's life-threatening.

A stove needs to meet a number of criteria. It must be capable of bringing water to a boil under the worst conditions you're likely to encounter, it must be small and light enough to pack, and it must be simple to operate. Stability is important too, particularly when using large pans.

FUELS

The availability of fuel in the areas you plan to visit may determine the stove you select. The choice is between liquid fuel (in the form of alcohol, kerosene, or white gas) and cartridges (containing butane or butane and propane).

Fuel consumption depends on the type of stove you have, the weather, and the type of cooking you do. If you cook three meals a day and use foods with long cooking times, you'll obviously use more fuel than someone who only boils water for a freeze-dried dinner at night.

White gas. White gas is the most efficient stove fuel—it lights easily and burns very hot. Automobile fuel is sometimes used, but it can quickly clog fuel jets (many stove makers state firmly that it shouldn't be used). These stoves should be run on specially refined fuel such as Coleman fuel. White gas is volatile, ignites easily if spilled, and requires a lot of care. In North America, it's the only fuel you can find just about anywhere.

White-gas stoves burn the fuel as it's vaporized, which means that it has to be pressurized. In the simplest models, the fuel is transmitted from the tank to the burner via a wick that leads into the fuel line. These stoves have to be preheated or primed before they're lit, so that the fuel can vaporize before passing through the jet. Models with pressure pumps make the stove easier to light.

Because they burn pressurized fuel, these stoves can flare badly during lighting, so care is needed if they're used in a tent. They operate best when one-half to three-quarters full, and they should never be completely filled, since the fuel can't expand to pressurize the stove.

White-gas stoves have two types of burners: roarer and ported. The roarer uses a stream of vaporized fuel that is pushed out of the jet, ignites, and hits a burner plate that spreads it out into a ring of flame. Not surprisingly, they're noisy. In ported burners, the flames come out of a ring of jets, just like a kitchen gas range. Ported burners are much quieter. Neither type is more efficient than the other, although ported ones are easier to control and thus better for simmering.

Butane and propane. Light, clean, simple-to-use cartridge stoves are the choice of many kayakers. The fuel is liquid petroleum gas, kept under pressure in a sealed cartridge. The most popular version is pure butane, which is relatively cheap but sometimes difficult to find. Because of the cartridge's low pressure (necessary because its walls are thin to keep the weight down), the butane won't vaporize in temperatures much below 40 degrees F.

As the cartridge empties and the pressure drops, its burning rate falls until it won't bring water to a boil. Cartridges with a mixture of butane and propane work better in below-freezing temperatures because propane vaporizes at a much lower temperature than butane. Propane, however, is volatile and requires heavy, thick-walled containers. Lightweight cartridges are usually 85 percent butane and 15 percent propane.

All cartridge stoves have quiet, ported burners. The heat output is easily adjusted, making them excellent for simmering, but the flame must be protected from the wind. Most come with small windshields, but you may need a separate windshield in windy conditions. There are two types of cartridges: those with a self-sealing valve that allows you to remove the cartridge at any time, and those in which the cartridge must be left on the stove until empty.

Kerosene. Kerosene is the traditional stove fuel. It's easily obtained and reasonably cheap, and it burns hot. Kerosene won't ignite easily, so it's safer than white gas if spilled. Consequently, it's also more difficult to light, usually requiring a separate priming fuel such as solid-fuel tablets or paste. Kerosene tends to flare during lighting, so it should always be ignited outside a tent. It's messy, stains badly, leaves a strong odor, and takes a long time to evaporate, but many kayakers swear by it.

The flame of a kerosene stove is controlled by opening a valve and releasing some of the pressure. These stoves have noisy roarer burners and are relatively heavy. Although the flame is powerful and most models have small windshields to protect the burners, their efficiency can be increased by using a full windshield in breezy conditions.

Alcohol. Fuel for alcohol stoves is available as denatured alcohol or marine stove fuel. It can be hard to find (look for it in hardware stores and backpacking shops) and expensive. It's the only fuel not derived from petroleum and the only one burned nonpressurized as a liquid, which makes it safer. It's clean, too, evaporating quickly if spilled. For these reasons, it's a good fuel if you'll be cooking regularly in the tent. But it's not a hot fuel, producing only half as much heat as the same weight of gasoline or kerosene.

Alcohol stoves can be set up quickly and have little that can go wrong; the only maintenance needed is to prick the jets occasionally. They're silent and safe, but you need to be careful when using one in daylight, because the flame is invisible. Because a full burner lasts only half an hour, the stove must be refilled often, and inadvertently filling a still-burning stove must be avoided.

FUEL CONTAINERS

There are many plastic and metal fuel bottles available. Plastic ones are fine for alcohol, but metal bottles are better for volatile fuels such as gasoline or kerosene. Fuel bottles must be sturdy, and they need a well-sealed, leakproof cap. Almost standard are the cylindrical Swiss-made Sigg bottles, which are extremely tough.

It's almost impossible to fill small fuel tanks directly from fuel bottles without spilling. A number of ingenious devices have been developed. One has a small plastic spout inserted in one side and a tiny hole drilled in the other. By placing a finger over the hole, the flow can be controlled.

SAFETY AND MAINTENANCE

All stoves are potentially dangerous and should be used cautiously. Before you light a stove, always check that attachments to fuel tanks or cartridges are secure, tank caps and fuel bottle tops are tight, and controls are turned off. Carefully study and practice the instructions that come with the stove.

Stoves are most dangerous during lighting, when they can flare badly. For this reason, never hold your head over the stove when you light it. Do not light a stove that's close to any flammable material, particularly your tent. Light it in open air whenever possible, even if this means placing it in the rain and bringing it inside the tent when it's burning.

A stove should also be refilled with care, after you've made sure that there are no burning candles, other lit stoves, or campfires nearby. This applies whether you're changing a butane cartridge or pouring fuel into a white-gas stove tank. Refuel outside the tent in case of spillage.

Overheating of cartridges or fuel tanks is another potential hazard. Make sure that enough air flows around the tank or cartridge and that the windscreen doesn't completely surround the stove. To avoid overheating, don't use rocks to stabilize stoves, and if you have large pans that overhang the burner, check periodically to see if too much heat is being reflected off the pans onto the tank.

Another real threat when using a stove inside a tent is carbon monoxide poisoning, which can be fatal. All stoves consume oxygen and give off this odorless, colorless gas, so ventilation is required.

Most stoves need little maintenance. Except for those with built-in self-cleaning needles, the jets of a stove may need cleaning with the thin wire stove-prickers that come with most models. Rubber seals on tank caps and cartridge attachment points should be checked periodically, lubricated if necessary, and replaced if worn.

ACCESSORIES

All stoves need a windscreen to function efficiently. Whatever windscreen you use, it should extend well above the burner to be effective.

To simplify the lighting of white-gas stoves, especially in cold weather, there's a small pump you can purchase to replace the fuel cap, but it must be used carefully to avoid overpressurizing the tank. Kerosene stoves need to be primed, and there are various flammable pastes for that purpose.

A recent innovation is a heat exchanger, which is a corrugated aluminum collar that fits around the stove and reduces boiling time by directing more heat up the sides of the pan.

FIRE STARTERS

Matches are essential for lighting fires and starting stoves, and it's a good idea to carry several boxes of strike-anywhere matches, each sealed in a small plastic bag. Waterproof match containers are also available. The likelihood of several boxes kept in different places becoming soaked is remote, but it can happen, so carrying an emergency fire starter of some kind is a good idea. A box of waterproof and windproof matches is ideal.

An alternative to matches is a cigarette lighter. Just the spark from a lighter ignites white-gas and butane stoves (though not kerosene or alcohol), and if the lighter gets wet, it's easily dried.

More esoteric fire starters are also available. Flint and magnesium ones work off chippings scraped from a magnesium block, and the chippings are ignited by sparks caused by drawing a knife across a flint. Another model has a brass "match" that lights a gasoline-soaked wick when struck. Carrying one of these models is recommended on remote trips.

UTENSILS

Cooking habits will determine the amount of kitchen gear you take. One advantage of minimal cooking is that it requires minimal tools.

Pans. Many stoves come with pans and windshields designed specifically for that stove. Tight-fitting lids are important, because they help water boil faster. Many lids are designed to double as frying pans, but most don't work very well, and a separate nonstick frying pan is better.

Pot grabs. Far superior to fixed pot handles are simple two-piece pot grabs that clamp onto the edge of the pan when the handles are pressed together. Not all are of good quality; some of the thin aluminum ones soon

---

ACROSS THE ATLANTIC

In 1956 a German named Hannes Lindemann crossed the Atlantic Ocean alone in a 17-foot folding kayak. It took him seventy-two days. His diet consisted mostly of evaporated milk and raw fish, but he allowed himself one can of beer a day. Along the way, he encountered tremendous storms and was nearly capsized on several occasions by huge porpoises. His military surplus sextants were lost at sea, and he finished the trip by dead reckoning. He was the only kayaker ever to be featured on the cover of *Life* magazine. Amazingly, Lindemann may have found the journey a little anticlimactic: The previous year he had crossed the Atlantic in a 23-foot canoe.

An English translation of his book *Alone at Sea* (previously available only in German) is now available from Western Folding Kayak Center, 6155 Mt. Aukum Rd., Somerset, CA 95684, (530) 626-8647.

distort and twist out of shape. To make tight-fitting lids easy to lift off pans, put the lids on upside down with the rims pointing upward.

Mugs. Plastic mugs are light and cheap but not very durable; they soon develop uncleanable scratches and cracks. They also retain tastes, which relegates them to one type of liquid. Mugs made of Lexan plastic are better: They don't retain tastes and are unbreakable.

The alternative to plastic is stainless steel (aluminum retains heat, so it's less practical). Stainless steel remains cool, doesn't taint, doesn't scratch, and is long-lasting. The classic is the Sierra Club cup with its shallow profile and wire handle.

Eating utensils. Lexan plastic also works for cutlery, but it discolors and can be broken. Metal lasts much longer.

WATER PURIFICATION

A kayak trip by definition involves water, but the problem is deciding whether it's safe to drink. Water clarity is, unfortunately, not an indication of purity. Even the most sparkling, crystal-clear mountain stream may be unsafe to drink. Invisible contaminants include a wide variety of microorganisms that cause diarrhea and dysentery—sometimes mild, sometimes severe. Giardiasis, which causes a virulent stomach disorder curable only by antibiotics, has received the most attention.

Giardiasis is caused by the protozoan *Giardia lamblia*, which lives in the intestines of humans and animals. It's transferred through water in the form of cysts and in feces (another reason to always situate toilets well away from water). The symptoms of giardiasis appear a few weeks after ingestion, and they include diarrhea, stomachache, bloating, and nausea. Because these occur in other stomach disorders as well, only a stool analysis can confirm infection. If you're unlucky enough to become infected with giardiasis, prescription antibiotics can cure the disease. However, prevention is preferable.

Water can be purified by boiling, treatment with chemicals, and filtration. Boiling is the surest way to kill dangerous organisms, but it's impractical—except perhaps for water used in camp—because it uses fuel and takes time. Iodine and chlorine tablets are lightweight and simple to use, but neither is fully effective; iodine is better than chlorine, however. Both make the water taste unpleasant, so you'll want to add fruit-flavored mixes to make it drinkable. Potable Aqua is a common brand of iodine tablets, but they have a limited shelf life, so you should buy a fresh supply at least annually. Iodine crystals are reputedly more effective than tablets; kits containing iodine crystals, thermometers, and instructions can be purchased at most outdoor stores. Use iodine carefully; too much will poison you.

Filtration is probably the best treatment. There are a number of lightweight, handheld systems available; many have replaceable charcoal-based filters that screen out pesticides and chemicals (which boiling won't do), as well as microorganisms larger than 0.4 micron. The most expensive of these filters is the Swiss-made Katadyn Pocket Water Filter, whose silver-quartz-impregnated ceramic filter screens out organisms larger than 0.2 micron.

Water bottles. Water containers are available in a wide variety of shapes, sizes, and materials. Aluminum keeps liquids cool in summer, but unless it's lacquered inside, it contaminates water containing drink mixes. The heavy-duty Nalgene brand plastic bottles have wide mouths for easy filling and caps that don't leak. Special insulated covers are available.

For camp use, you'll need a larger water container. A lot of kayakers take along the ubiquitous 5-gallon water containers made of collapsible plastic, but they spring holes quickly. More sturdy are water bags with plastic inner bladders and tough nylon outer bags.

In really cold weather, thermos-type flasks can be useful, the best ones made of unbreakable stainless steel. If you fill one before leaving camp, you can enjoy hot drinks during the day. This eliminates the need to stop and fire up the stove.

ANIMAL PROOFING

In some areas, animals can be a threat to your food supply, and it takes a little ingenuity to foil their efforts. If you're camped near trees, hang your food bag from a low branch to protect it from animals. In areas where bears raid campsites, food bags need to be hung at least 12 feet above the ground and 10 feet away from the trunk of the tree. They should also be 6 feet below any branch.

There are various ways of doing this, all requiring 50 feet or more of nylon line. The simplest method is to tie a rock to the end of the line, throw it over a branch about 20 feet above the ground and 10 feet from the trunk, haul up the food until the bottom of the bag is 12 feet or more high, then tie off the line around the trunk of the tree.

With smaller trees, you may have to suspend food bags between two trees about 25 feet apart, which involves throwing one end of the weighted line over a branch, tying it off, and then repeating the process with the other end over a branch of the second tree. Keep the line between the two trees within reach so you can tie the food bag to it. Then haul the

ZEN AND THE ART OF PADDLING

It's not your typical kayak book, but *The Starship and the Canoe*, by Kenneth Brower (New York: Holt, Rinehart, 1973), is the true story of an eccentric visionary who builds gigantic kayaks to cruise the Pacific Northwest seas and his astrophysicist father, who dreams of building a nuclear-powered spaceship the size of Chicago. The kayak involved is a resurrection of the Aleut kayak that Russian fur hunters named *baidarka*. This is the compelling story of two men, two arks, and two views of humankind's destiny.

bag up until it is halfway between the trees and about 12 feet off the ground.

In a few areas, animals have learned that breaking a line rewards them with a bag of food. In these places, neither of these methods works. Instead, you must use a counterbalance system, which involves throwing the line over a branch that is at least 25 feet high, tying a food bag to the end of the line, and hauling it up to the branch. You then tie a second food bag, or a bag of rocks if you don't have enough food, to the other end of the line. Then heave the second bag into the air, or use a stick to pull down the other bag, so that both bags end up 12 feet or more above the ground and 10 feet from the tree trunk. If you leave a loop of line at the top of one of the bags, you can hook it with a stick to pull the bags down in the morning.

If you camp far from trees, store food at least 100 yards away from your tent in airtight plastic bags. Animals are attracted to food by smell, so they may consider items such as toothpaste, soap, insect repellent, sunscreen, food-stained clothing, dishrags, and dirty pots and pans to be food. Hang them with your food, and keep them out of your tent.

WILDERNESS CUISINE

How scientific do you have to be when selecting foods for a kayak trip? Not very, as long as you use good sense and plan reasonably well-balanced meals. What works at home will work in the wilds, with one exception: calories. You'll need lots of them—4,000 a day if you're paddling hard. Fortunately, you don't need to be too exacting in determining nutritional value, but it's important to balance your daily intake of foods.

Carbohydrates. Carbohydrates provide quick energy and should supply at least 50 percent of your daily caloric requirement. Foods that contain carbohydrates include breads, cereals, honey, jam, dehydrated fruits, and candy.

Fats. Fats contain about twice as many calories per pound as carbohydrates and are the body's major source of stored energy. Generally, fats should provide about 20 to 25 percent of your calories, and during a rigorous trip, even more. Foods containing fats are margarine, cooking oil, nuts, peanut butter, cheese, bacon, and sausage.

Proteins. Wilderness kayaking is a strenuous activity, so you'll need more protein than normal: a hearty breakfast of oat or wheat cereal and milk; a lunch that includes cheese, beef jerky, peanut butter, or sausage; and a supper that contains meat or beans.

WEIGHT AND BULK

Weight and bulk don't matter much on one- or two-night jaunts, but they can be a concern on longer trips. Fresh and canned foods are bulky and heavy, so dried foods are the best choice. The simplest method of drying food is under the hot sun. Because this doesn't remove as much moisture as other methods, it's not used for many foods, though some fruits are sun-dried. Air-drying, whereby the food is spun in a drum or arranged on trays through which hot air is blown, produces dehydrated foods. But reconstituted dehydrated foods have a reputation for poor taste.

The most expensive means of extracting water from food is freeze-drying, whereby food is frozen so quickly that the moisture turns to ice. The food is then placed in a low-temperature vacuum, where the ice turns

---

ARCTIC VOYAGE

Among the Inuit people, Victoria Jason became known as the *kabloona*, the Inuktitut word for stranger. In the summer of 1991, Jason, a novice kayaker, began an arctic voyage that would eventually entail 4,500 miles and consume four summers. Despite a number of lingering medical problems, Jason set out from Churchill, Manitoba, and paddled the first half of the journey to Gjoa Haven on King William Island. She then completed the circle by starting at Fort Providence on Great Slave Lake, heading up the Mackenzie River to its mouth, and traveling along the coast through the Beaufort Sea back to Gjoa Haven. The tale is contained in her book *Kabloona in the Yellow Kayak* (Winnipeg: Turnstone Press, 1995).

directly into vapor without passing through a liquid state. Freeze-dried food is costly, but it tastes better. Because the food can be cooked before being freeze-dried, you only need to add boiling water.

To supplement your dried foods, you'll need lots of calories on a rigorous outing, and that means extra bread, peanut butter, margarine, nuts, cereals, and cheese. The food you take should be lightweight, slow to spoil, easy to prepare, and stable in hot weather.

PACKING SUGGESTIONS

Organizing your meals before you hit the water will repay itself many times over. To eliminate confusion and shorten preparation times, package each meal as a complete unit. Remove all unnecessary cardboard and paper wrappers to save weight, space, and the amount of trash you'll have to pack out. Label the bags "B-l" (breakfast on the first day), "L-2" (lunch on the second day), and so forth.

Sugar, flour, drink mixes, and other pourable solids are best premeasured and placed in sturdy plastic Ziploc bags. Breakable and crushable items, such as crackers, cheese, and candy bars, should be packed inside rigid cardboard containers, which can be burned as their contents are consumed. Liquids are best carried in plastic bottles with screw-cap lids; Nalgene brand containers, available at most camping stores, are the most reliable.

COOKING TIMES

The time food takes to cook affects the amount of fuel you need to carry and the amount of time you'll have to wait. When you're exhausted and hungry and a storm is raging all around, knowing that your dinner will be ready in five minutes rather than thirty can be important. As you gain altitude, water takes longer to boil; at 5,000 feet, the cooking time is twice that at sea level.

Many foods, from instant soup to eat-from-the-packet freeze-dried meals, don't require any cooking, just boiling water and a quick stir. But they usually don't taste as good as meals that require a little simmering. Most meals need five to ten minutes, a good compromise between speed and taste.

Cooking times for some dried foods can be reduced by presoaking. This works with vegetables, meat, and legumes, but not pasta or rice. Some kayakers soak food in a capped bottle during the day so that it's ready for cooking at night.

SUGGESTED MENUS

Food suitable for kayaking can be found in supermarkets, health-food stores, and outdoor shops. Prices are lowest in supermarkets, which usually have all the foods you need, perhaps with the exception of freeze-dried meals. Check cooking times carefully; one packet of soup may take five minutes to cook, another twenty-five. Health-food stores have a wider variety of cereals, dried fruits, and grain bars than do supermarkets, although the number of supermarkets selling these foods is increasing. You'll find foods specifically made for backpackers and mountaineers in outdoor stores; these are lightweight and low in bulk, though expensive. Highly recommended is Linda Daniel's *Kayak Cookery* (Birmingham, AL: Menasha Ridge Press, 1997).

Lightweight meals. Meals on kayak trips can be as simple as you wish to make them. Many kayakers prefer lightweight meals because they allow them to spend more time on the water. Here's a sampling of some lightweight, simple menus.

Breakfast. Regardless of the weather, tea, instant coffee, or hot chocolate is a nice way to start the day. The main meal for a lightweight breakfast could be one or more of the following:

- Instant hot cereals, such as oatmeal or cream of wheat
- Cold cereals, such as granola or Grape Nuts, using powdered milk or vacuum-packed milk that doesn't need refrigeration
- Freeze-dried breakfasts, available at backpacking and outdoor stores
- Snack foods that do not require cooking, such as cheese, crackers, salami, jerky, nuts, or dried fruit

Lunch. To save time, lunch typically is not cooked. Some kayakers schedule a special day when they cook lunch, but this usually takes too much time to be done every day. It is, however, a good idea to bring some extra hot drinks or soup mixes for cold, rainy days. Here are some suggestions for a lightweight lunch:

- Bread for sandwiches
- Salami
- Canned fish (tuna, salmon, kippers, sardines)
- Canned meat (sandwich spreads, chicken, beef)
- Jerky
- Crackers
- Cheese
- Dried fruits

- Various types of candies (sugar or honey)
- Peanut butter
- Granola
- Nuts
- Gorp (mixture of raisins, nuts, chocolate chips)

Supper. Soup or hot drinks are a quick predinner warm-up. The main course can consist of a freeze-dried dinner, the lightest and most convenient meal there is. The best types of freeze-dried dinners are those to which you add hot water, then wait several minutes before eating. Unfortunately, the convenience of freeze-dried dinners comes with a price. You can put together many fine, nutritional, lightweight meals by buying products at your local supermarket, where various dehydrated foods and convenience meals are available, such as beef Stroganoff or chicken tetrazzini. For simplicity, most lightweight meals are cooked in one pot, though some people prepare separate dishes.

Luxurious meals. A lot of paddlers find eating to be an important part of their outdoor experience, so they don't mind spending a little time and effort in the kitchen. The results can be extraordinary.

Breakfast. A good warm-up for a luxurious breakfast is a hot drink of coffee, tea, or cocoa. Some people like to serve fruit juices along with the main meal. The meal can consist of one or more of the following:

- Eggs—scrambled, fried, boiled, or poached
- Omelet
- Bacon
- Quiche
- Egg and potato casserole
- Hash browns
- Pancakes
- French toast
- Fruit

Lunch. Since cooking is time-consuming, most lunches are served cold. Typical items include the following:

- Bread, rolls, or bagels
- Lunch meats (turkey, beef, corned beef, bologna)
- Salami or sausage
- Cheese
- Peanut butter
- Jam

- Tuna fish
- Pickles
- Mayonnaise, mustard, catsup
- Fresh fruit
- Candy and cookies

Supper. Just about everything goes for supper on luxurious-style trips. To keep food cold, use soft-sided insulated coolers, which are easier to pack inside the kayak.

To warm up after a long day on the water, start with a soup. Use packaged mixes or canned soups, or even start from scratch. The primary course can center around a meat dish such as steak, hamburgers, pork chops, or chicken, or it can be vegetarian. Various salads (lettuce, bean, and potato) and fruits balance out the main meal, and bread or biscuits can also be served. Dessert—pie, cake, or brownies—or popcorn is often made later in the evening when everyone is gathered around the fire.

SNACKS
A staple snack food is that mixture of dried fruit, nuts, and seeds known as trail mix or gorp (good old raisins and peanuts). The basic mix consists of peanuts and raisins, but more sophisticated mixes include bits of dried fruit (favorites are papaya, pineapple, and dates), a variety of other nuts, coconut, chocolate chips, sunflower and sesame seeds, granola, and anything else you like.

Savory snacks such as crispbread or crackers and a cheese or vegetable spread make a pleasant contrast. Spreads that come in easy-to-use squeeze tubes are especially convenient. Or you can transfer spreads into squeeze tubes designed for reuse.

SPICES
There are various ways to enhance the taste of any meal. Adding herbs and spices such as garlic powder, cloves, curry, chili powder, or black pepper helps. Margarine, cheese, and milk powder add calories as well as taste. Packets of soup can provide flavoring or be part of a meal with pasta and rice.

11

THE BEDROOM

It has been a long day of paddling, you're tired, and there's nothing like pulling into a warm, comfortable camp. A campsite, if you've taken the effort to select the right sleeping bag and tent, can be a place of respite, a virtual home away from home—and with a much better view.

SLEEPING BAGS

The sleeping bag is a simple concept that performs an unglamorous but invaluable function—it traps warm air to keep the body from cooling down at night. How well a sleeping bag performs this task is largely the result of its materials and construction.

FILL

The biggest factor in choosing a sleeping bag is the type of insulation, or fill, it has—either down (goose or duck) or synthetic. The ideal material is lightweight, warm, compact, durable, quick-drying, and very soft. Unfortunately, the ideal fill doesn't exist, so a few compromises have to be made, depending on when and where you camp, the shelter you use, and the chances of getting your bag wet.

Before DuPont launched Fiberfill II in the mid-1970s, synthetic-filled sleeping bags were far too heavy and bulky for kayaking. Since then, a host of good synthetic fills have appeared, and kayakers can now choose from a variety of lightweight and compact bags. There are two basic types of synthetic fill: chopped fibers and continuous filaments. Chopped fibers are short sections of fill, often hollow inside. Continuous filaments are long strands of fiber. Polarguard is the only continuous filament, but there are many versions of chopped fibers, the best known being Quallofil and Hollofil II. Which type of fill is better matters less than the quality of the bag as a whole.

Synthetic fills cost less than down, are easy to care for, and resist moisture. The synthetics are not, however, warm when wet, as some manufacturers claim. Synthetic fills dry fairly quickly because they are nonabsorbent—an obvious advantage on a kayak trip. Because the fill doesn't collapse when saturated, much of its ability to trap warm air is retained. When compared with a wet down bag, a wet synthetic bag will start to warm you in a shorter time, as long as it's protected from the wind. Compared with down, the disadvantages of synthetic fills are a shorter life span, less comfort, more bulk, and greater weight.

The lightest, warmest, most comfortable, and most durable sleeping bags are those made of down. These bags are best when weight and bulk are critical, because no synthetic fiber has down's insulating ability. Down has its disadvantages, however. It must be kept dry, as it loses virtually all its insulating qualities when wet. It's also very absorbent, and it takes a long time to dry. Drying out a down bag in bad weather is almost impossible—only the hot sun or a tumble dryer will do the job. Keeping the bag dry on a kayak trip means packing it in a completely waterproof bag and always using shelter when it rains. Down bags also require frequent airing to remove moisture picked up from humid air or from your body during the night.

Down comes in different grades and types. Pure down is usually at least 85 percent down, the remainder being small feathers that are impossible to separate (the more stalks you feel, the higher the percentage of feathers in it). Goose down is regarded as warmer than duck down; it's also more expensive. The more space the down can fill, the higher its quality, as its thickness, or loft, determines its warmth. The volume filled by one ounce of down gives a measurement called fill-power; most pure down has a fill-power between 500 and 650 cubic inches per ounce.

SHELL MATERIALS

Nylon is the best material for containing the fill of a sleeping bag. It's lightweight, durable, wind and water resistant, nonabsorbent, and quick drying. The latest nylons are comfortable against the skin, making them suitable for the inner as well as the outer shell. In the past, nylons felt cold and clammy, so many campers chose cotton or polyester-cotton interiors, even though they're heavier, slower drying, and harder to keep clean. The new nylons, however, have a pleasant feel and the ability to spread moisture over the surface, which speeds up evaporation.

A breathable and waterproof outer shell, such as Gore-Tex, provides good water resistance, but it adds to the weight and cost and will leak unless its seams are sealed. A few models come with special inner liners designed to increase warmth by reflecting body heat.

SHAPE AND SIZE

The most efficient bag is one that traps warm air close to the body. A sleeping bag that's too wide or too long won't keep you as warm as a properly sized one. A bag that's too small won't keep you warm in spots where you press against the shell and flatten the fill.

A roomy bag has lots of dead air space. Most bags reduce this dead space by tapering from head to foot, and they have hoods to prevent heat loss. The result is called a mummy bag, and it's the standard for high-performance sleeping bags used in cooler weather. Many kayakers, however, object to the confines of a mummy bag, so they choose a semirectangular bag, which is warmer than a rectangular bag but less restricting than a mummy.

CONSTRUCTION

The method used to hold fill in the sleeping bag determines how efficient the bag will be. Fill migrates unless it's held in channels; to create these channels, the inner and outer shells of a bag are stitched together. The simplest way of doing this is sewn-through stitching, but heat escapes through the stitch lines, and the oval channels created don't allow the fill to expand fully. To reduce this heat loss, the inner and outer shells can be connected by short walls of fabric to make boxes, called box-wall or slant-wall construction. Virtually all cold-weather down bags have these internal walls.

This construction can't be used on synthetic bags because the fill is fixed in layers, so two other techniques are used. In double-layer construction, two, sometimes three, sewn-through layers are used, with the stitch lines offset to eliminate cold spots. In single-layer construction, slanted layers of overlapping fiber are sewn to both the inner and the outer shells. This is supposedly lighter and allows the fill to loft more easily.

Whatever the internal construction, a bag's channels are usually divided by lengthwise side baffles, which prevent the fill from ending up on the top or bottom of the bag. Some bags, usually lightweight down ones, dispense with side baffles on the theory that it might be useful at times to redistribute the fill. To prevent fill compression, the outer shell on many bags is cut larger than the inner; this is known as a differential cut.

DESIGN

A good sleeping bag hood fits closely around the head, and it should have a draw cord with toggles to permit easy adjustment. Bags used in below-freezing temperatures usually have large hoods in which you can bury all but your nose. To prevent drafts, an insulated collar is often a feature. To keep your feet warm, a sleeping bag should have a shaped foot section; if the two halves of the bag are simply sewn together, your feet will compress the fill.

Zippers allow you to regulate temperature, and couples can zip two bags together to make one big bag. To prevent heat loss, zippers should have insulated baffles running down the inside.

LINERS

Sleeping bag liners are available in cotton, polypropylene, silk, pile, and coated nylon. Cotton is heavy and slow drying; polypropylene liners, which absorb less moisture, make more sense. Pile liners, though bulky, can upgrade a bag for colder conditions, and silk is very light and compact. Coated nylon liners can be used to form a vapor barrier that keeps in moisture and stops evaporative heat loss. In dry, cold conditions, especially when the temperature is well below freezing, a vapor-barrier liner (VBL) can add a surprising amount of warmth.

RATINGS

Rating sleeping bags for warmth is difficult, because there's no standard system. Most companies use ratings that give either the lowest temperature or a range in which the bag will be comfortable. No rating system, however, can account for different metabolic rates. Some people are warm sleepers, some cold. Putting on more clothes is an obvious solution when you wake up in the night feeling chilled, but a carbohydrate snack can also help. If you camp without a tent, you'll need a warmer bag; using a sleeping pad also makes a big difference in both comfort and warmth.

PADS AND PILLOWS

For comfort and insulation, a sleeping bag needs a pad underneath it. There are basically two types: closed-cell and self-inflating. Air mattresses and open-cell foam are still available but are not widely used. Closed-cell pads are light, reasonably cheap, and hard-wearing, but they're bulky and don't add much padding. More comfortable is a self-inflating model like the Therm-a-Rest, which has a nylon shell bonded to a core of open-cell foam that expands when the valve is opened (a few puffs speed up the process). The only problem with these pads is their slipperiness; to solve this, many campers buy pad covers or apply special sprays.

For a pillow, some kayakers use a pile or down jacket, perhaps packed into a stuffsack. If you prefer something more comfortable, there are a number of lightweight camp pillows available.

TENTS

Selecting the right tent isn't as easy as it might appear, since they come in an almost limitless variety of shapes and sizes. Seek good advice from a salesperson, and carefully study the outdoor gear catalogs. To narrow the field, you need to ask a few questions:

- When and where will it be used?
- How many must it sleep?
- How critical is weight?

Then, issues of price and personal choice come into play.

Because a tent's main purpose is to protect against wind and rain, it must be windproof and waterproof. It should also be lightweight and compact when packed, yet strong and durable enough to withstand severe weather. Like rainwear, tents must repel rain while letting condensation escape. The moisture given off by the human body overnight is considerable. The problem is minimized by two layers—a breathable inner layer and a waterproof outer layer, or flysheet. Moisture passes through the inner fabric and is then carried away by the flow of air circulating between the two layers. Condensation occurs on the inside of the flysheet, where it runs to the ground.

DESIGN

Since the advent of dome tents in the early 1970s, designers have created a bewildering array of tent shapes, some of them quite elaborate. These developments have led to tents that are lighter, roomier, tougher, and more durable than ever.

Dome tents. Before flexible tent poles appeared, all designs were variations on the standard ridge tent, a solid structure still popular with many kayakers. As good as traditional tents are, flexible-pole models are superior. Their steep sides and curved roofs give more usable space, and the self-supporting ones can be moved to a more suitable site after they've been erected.

Dome tents have flexible poles that cross each other at some point. They are the roomiest tents available, and most of them are self-supporting. There are two kinds: geodesic and cross-over-pole. Geodesic domes are complex structures in which four or more poles cross at several points. With cross-over-pole domes, two or three poles cross at the apex to give a spacious tent that is lighter than but not as stable as the geodesic type.

Traditional tents. A lot of kayakers still prefer the traditional design of a large wall tent with its angled roof, often called an A-frame tent. One model has an entire side that can be opened, either with or without a mosquito netting. The advantages of this versatile tent are obvious: increased ventilation and better views. Many are made of canvas, which renders them fairly heavy and bulky.

SIZE

Tents come in a wide range of sizes. You'll want enough inner height so that you can sit up and move around. You also need to consider the size of the tent's vestibule, if any. If you expect to cook and store gear there, it needs to be roomy.

MATERIALS

Most tents are made of nylon or polyester, and these are undoubtedly the most practical. Cotton canvas is heavy and absorbs moisture. Nylon absorbs little moisture, dries quickly, and is very light. The flysheets used to cover most tents are plastic coated to keep out rain. To prevent leaks, flysheet seams are often sealed with adhesive sealant, though some of the better ones come with fully taped seams.

Breathable fabrics can be used to combat condensation in tents as they do in clothing, and several models are made from Gore-Tex. These tents are easy to pitch because they have just one layer, but because the fabrics don't work well in larger tents, most models are small.

STABILITY

For three-season, sheltered-site camping, stability is not a major concern. For exposed sites and cold-weather camping, however, it's a prime consideration. The stability of a tent is determined by a host of factors—shape, materials, number of poles and how they're arranged, and number and position of guylines. Look for a tent with plenty of guylines and no large areas of unsupported material.

Stability, of course, is relative. Violent gales can shred the strongest tent. In extreme winds, a sheltered site may be as important as the tent. When pitching the tent seems impossible because of high winds, it may be better to go on, even after dark, in search of a more protected area.

Poles. Poles can be rigid or flexible. They're usually made from aluminum, though some are made from fiberglass. Poles whose sections are linked by elastic shockcord are the most convenient. Tents with solid poles should be avoided, because their unlinked sections tend to come apart inside the tent sleeves.

Most poles are attached to the tent by threading them through nylon or mesh sleeves and then fixing the end into a grommet strip or tape loop.

A few models use clips or shockcord to hang the tent from the poles; these tents are faster to set up.

Stakes and guylines. Regardless of its claims, every tent requires some staking to hold it down in strong winds. Long, heavy stakes aren't necessary. Smaller aluminum stakes hold in most soils; for softer ground, you can carry a few V-angle stakes. Stakes are easy to misplace, so take two or three extra.

Depending on design, tents need guylines to keep them taut in a wind. To avoid confusion, different-colored guylines may be useful, especially when several are attached to the tent at the same point. To tighten the guylines, sliders are handy.

12

WILDERNESS LIVING

A lot of touring kayakers seem to take everything with them—and I do mean everything. The beauty is that the touring kayak can accommodate most of their desires. Other kayakers are less inclined toward taking it all, though they still like to pack those things that make them comfortable in their home away from home.

GEAR

SUNGLASSES

When you're camping on a stretch of water, there's a frequent problem—glare. Sunglasses can help relieve much of the discomfort and even potential damage to your eyes. Unfortunately, not all models do the job equally well. Optical experts agree that a good pair of sunglasses should provide 15 to 35 percent light transmission. Therefore, the lenses should absorb 65 to 85 percent of the rays striking them. Ultraviolet and infrared light transmission should be at least as low.

The manufacturer of the sunglasses you're considering should provide these specifications. If it doesn't, a rough method of determining visible light transmission is to look in a mirror. Lenses through which the eyes are easily visible are probably too light for proper glare protection.

Almost all lenses block some ultraviolet light, but not all control infrared. Unless the manufacturer provides this information, the buyer's safest investment is green or gray sunglasses, which are most likely to provide sufficient protection. They also provide the best color perception, because the human eye is sensitive to these wavelengths.

Mirrored sunglasses have a thin coating of steel alloy that reflects light off the front of the lenses, providing greater protection without the necessity for darker lenses. The drawback is that they can increase sunburn on the nose.

A kayak allows you to get away from it all.

Polarizing lenses eliminate glare from flat surfaces, but viewing objects from other angles diminishes the effect: At 90 degrees, virtually no glare is eliminated. This makes them a questionable investment.

Photochromic lenses, which automatically darken as the light increases, are designed to increase eye protection as the intensity of ultraviolet light increases. But they absorb few infrared rays.

Still another category is mountaineering sunglasses, which have extremely dark lenses and leather side shields. Caution should be used when selecting them: Their darkness may result in pupil dilation and thereby actually increase the ultraviolet light transmission to the eyes.

SUNSCREEN

Protecting your skin with sunscreen is a necessity on kayak trips, where the glare from the water intensifies the sun's rays. Among the many sunscreens on the market, choose those that don't wash off as quickly with water and sweat. All sunscreens have a sun protection factor (SPF) number; the higher the SPF, the more protection it provides. SPFs of 15 and above provide virtually total protection and are recommended for high

Wilderness travel provides a pleasant change of pace.

altitudes where ultraviolet light, the part of the spectrum that burns, is stronger. Brimmed hats are likewise important. Lips can suffer from windburn as well as sunburn, so a tube of lip balm can save days of pain.

BINOCULARS

It's amazing how few campers take binoculars and how often they regret it. Binoculars can be used for identifying birds, spotting mountain sheep, even determining whether to pull over for the day because the last campsite downstream has been taken.

Perhaps people think that binoculars are expensive; some undoubtedly are, but in reality, the price range is wide, with several good models costing less than a good rainsuit. Or perhaps the descriptive jargon, such as focal lengths and complex prisms, sounds too complicated, when in actuality, the basic specifications can be mastered in minutes.

Most binocular literature refers to two numbers: 7 x 35, for example. The first number refers to the magnification of the object. You would think that the greater the magnification the better, but the slightest hand tremor can distort the image of binoculars with a power of greater than 7 or 8. Generally, the greater the magnification, the narrower the field of view. The second number refers to the diameter of the front lenses in millimeters. The greater the number, the more light that's allowed to enter. But again, bigger is not necessarily better; unless you need night vision, there's little advantage in having a lens diameter greater than five times that of magnification. A number of good models have a factor of three, such as 8 x 24.

The binoculars you choose should be light, compact, comfortable, and water resistant. Price is determined by lens quality, coatings, and prism setups. Some operating features vary: Some users prefer center focusing, which allows quick refocusing at short range and is best for bird-watching; others like the individual focusing of each eyepiece, said to be more durable. Even wide-angle binoculars are available. The number of models on the market is overwhelming, and with a little research, you shouldn't have any trouble finding what's best for you.

A coastal kayaker can experience the marine environment like few others.

TARPS

Some kayakers use tarps for shelter in an attempt to cut down on their load. This works fine if the weather—and absence of mosquitoes—allows it. Even those who take tents find a tarp useful for shade in midday or as a dining canopy at night. A number of models are made in sophisticated geometric designs that look attractive and shed the wind nicely. The key to a good tarp setup is lots of nylon line.

LIGHTS

Unless you're camping near the Arctic Circle, you'll probably need some kind of area light. Miniature versions of the traditional Coleman lantern are available. Most lanterns work on white gas, though there are propane and battery-operated models as well. The amount of light provided is astonishing. Those looking for a lightweight alternative have a choice of identical lanterns, only smaller. An even more compact option is the candle lantern, though the amount of light given off is considerably less.

For directional light, there is an almost limitless variety of flashlights in many sizes. Many kayakers prefer headlamps, which leave the hands free for cooking and other tasks. Carrying spare batteries and bulbs is always a good idea.

LOUNGE CHAIRS

Even the purists have come to recognize the benefits of a camp chair, and their use has become ubiquitous among touring kayakers. The new designs are so light that weight and bulk are hardly issues, especially since many are used in conjunction with sleeping pads.

CAMP SHOWERS

The camp shower is another invention that has encouraged camping among those who are loath to give up their luxuries back home. No longer is it necessary to forgo a hot shower simply because you're in the wilderness. Leave the shower (typically black plastic) in the sun all day, and the results that evening are magic.

WATER BUCKETS

A number of collapsible water buckets are available, and they are useful for hauling water to camp and as dishwashing buckets. Choose the sturdier models for reliability.

TOOLS

In this department are knives, axes, saws, shovels, and a number of other ingenious tools. The ax, saw, and shovel are important parts of the camping mystique, and a lot of people carry them for that reason alone. Even with the compact models designed for camping, many kayakers find their use too rare to justify taking. It's a matter of choice.

Knives are obviously important for the kitchen, where most campers prefer a sheath knife because of its size and convenience. A lot of campers pack along a folding knife as well, especially those of the Swiss Army variety, with their screwdrivers, files, magnifying glasses, and so forth.

The latest development is the multitool, like the Leatherman, which contains pliers, knife blades, files, screwdrivers, and wire cutter in one compact package. Regardless of how often they're used, they look good strapped to one's belt.

OTHER GEAR

Most campers like to take along a few other items.

Camera. The choice of cameras is wide, and a number of rugged, compact models designed specifically for camping are available.

Fishing gear. A lot of kayakers are just fishermen in disguise. The variety of compact rods and reels for backcountry travel is impressive.

Field guides. The more you know about the flora and fauna of an area, the more you'll appreciate it.

Many kayakers take along all the comforts of home.

Hiking boots. Hiking is one of camping's best diversions, and many kayak campers take along a pair of lightweight hiking boots to partake.

Pack towel. This ingenious camping device serves as a bath towel but is so absorbent that it's a fraction of the size. It's also extremely quick-drying.

The world opens up when you can paddle to it.

CAMPING SUPPLIES

A number of companies offer catalogs featuring lightweight camping equipment of interest to kayakers:

Campmor, Box 700, Saddle River, NJ 07458, (800) 226-7667

L. L. Bean, Inc., Freeport, ME 04033, (800) 221-4221 (request "Sporting Specialties" catalog)

Piragis Northwoods Company, 105 N. Central Ave., Ely, MN 55731, (800) 223-6565

Recreational Equipment, Inc. (REI), 1700 45th St. East, Sumner, WA 98390, (800) 426-4840

Hiker's compass. This is handy for side hikes and to follow one's route on a topographic map. Also useful are the map wheels, which give distance.

Games. There are now board games made for kayakers looking to while away the evening hours around the campfire or inside the tent during a rainstorm.

Musical instruments. Flutes, kazoos, and even larger musical instruments can be taken to provide entertainment at night.

Books. More than likely you'll be too busy, but should you get stuck in a storm, it's nice to have something to read.

WEATHER WATCHING

It's a great day on the water—sun shining, birds chirping, fish jumping, and all that—and then suddenly, everything breaks loose. As the gale-driven front bullies its way across the gray horizon, you find yourself paddling frantically to shore and running for cover, where you spend the day in a tent whose walls seem to compress as the day drags on.

If anything, weather is unpredictable. For that reason alone, it's important to consider weather not only in the planning of a trip but also once you're on the water. A good understanding of its volatile nature helps in packing the right clothing and also relates to such health and safety matters as rising water levels and the prevention of hypothermia, and perhaps heatstroke as well.

A kayaker, like a professional meteorologist, has a number of tools in his or her weather-predicting arsenal. Information about past conditions—monthly tables of previous temperatures, relative humidity, average rainfall, days without rain, and so forth—is helpful in the planning stages of a trip. Ranging from a month before the trip until the day you leave, the forecasts on the weather channel are an invaluable aid in making decisions on what camping gear and clothing you should bring.

Additionally, there's the in-the-field forecasting that inevitably comes while you're on the water. A casual forecast of "Certainly looks like rain to me" is sure to be countered with a more skeptical "I really don't think *that* cloud has any moisture in it." Obviously, there's nothing you can do to affect the weather, but the forces above should be observed, because they can have an impact on your plans.

The border between two air masses is known as a front, and the interactions between them is due to the weight of air. Cold, dry air is heavy; warm, moist air is light. These different weights cause variations in air pressures—the highs and the lows that weathercasters are always talking about. In simplest terms, rain and snow are just condensation that occurs when a warm, moist air mass rides over a heavy, cold one.

Logically, a front is deemed warm if the warmer subtropical air is advancing, and cold if the cold polar air is gaining ground. Most large storms are the result of what is known as an occluded front, which results when two fast-moving, cold air masses meet, restricting the warm air in size and lifting it completely off the ground.

Clouds are telltale signs of an imminent change in weather. If interpreted correctly, they can inform you about upper wind drift, precipitation levels, instability of fronts, and the speed of an oncoming change in weather. Clouds are convection currents made visible when the dew point is reached. The main cloud formations are the big, wispy cirrus; the layered stratus; and the massive cumulus. The terms *alto*, meaning "high," and *nimbus*, meaning "rain," further describe their formations.

The massive, mountainlike cumulus clouds—and in particular the altocumulus clouds, with their globular cloudlets that look like white paving stones—are the forerunners of a cold front, especially when followed by lower, denser clouds. They require immediate attention, because they appear only a few hours before a storm, thus giving little advance warning. However, the disturbance is usually short-lived.

The thin and wispy cirrus clouds, appearing like curls of hair extremely high in the air, are the earliest signs of an approaching warm front, usually giving plenty of notice, since they precede the front and its storm by eighteen to thirty-six hours. When these cirrus clouds merge into layered stratus clouds, and especially the lower and darker cirrostratus, a storm is almost assured.

What are the best warnings of an impending storm? The experts give three: (1) shifts in wind speed and direction, (2) changes in the sky's

GREAT RIVER OUTFITTERS

Weather forecasting is an important skill in any kayaker's arsenal.

appearance, and (3) variations in temperature, humidity, and pressure. As it turns out, the experts' advice is often consistent with folklore. The adage of "red sky at night, sailor's delight" is sometimes misleading, but that of "red sky at morning, sailor's take warning" is generally reliable. The movement of upper clouds tells the direction of the winds aloft; if it's greatly different from that of the winds below, a change in weather is usually in the cards.

Another accurate aid in from-the-hip forecasting is wind direction. As a general rule, if the wind is from the north or west, it means you're on the east side of an eastward-moving high-pressure area (away from the front), and fair weather is probable for the next several days. If the wind is from the east or south, you're on the east side of an eastward-moving low-pressure area (near the front), and wet conditions are likely. Because winds from any direction generally die down at night, any persistent or strong winds after sundown usually indicate that stormy weather is on the way.

Other weather folklore is contradictory, and some is downright bizarre. Leaving aside weather indicators related to insect behavior, arthritis, and even corns on the feet, some of the most common but least trustworthy have to do with phases and shapes of the moon. More reliable is the presence of a ring or halo around the moon or sun, formed by refraction through ice crystals in the clouds. These cirrostratus clouds are often seen when rain is approaching in less than twenty-four hours, but because these rings are also visible in rainless weather, they can be false alarms.

APPENDIX 1

FOR FURTHER READING

BOOKS

Burch, David. *Fundamentals of Kayak Navigation*. 2nd ed. Old Saybrook, CT: Globe Pequot Press, 1993.

Dowd, John. *Sea Kayaking: A Manual for Long-Distance Touring*. 2nd ed. Seattle: University of Washington Press, 1997.

Foster, Nigel. *Nigel Foster's Sea Kayaking*. Old Saybrook, CT: Globe Pequot Press, 1997.

Harrison, David. *Sea Kayaking Basics*. New York: Hearst Marine Books, 1993.

Hutchinson, Derek C. *The Complete Book of Sea Kayaking*. 4th ed. Old Saybrook, CT: Globe Pequot Press, 1994.

———— *Derek C. Hutchinson's Guide to Expedition Kayaking on Sea and Open Water*. 3rd ed. Old Saybrook, CT: Globe Pequot Press, 1995.

Seidman, David. *The Essential Sea Kayaker: A Complete Course for the Open Water Paddler*. Camden, ME: Ragged Mountain Press, 1992.

Washburne, Randel. *The Coastal Kayaker's Manual: A Complete Guide to Skills, Gear, and Sea Sense*. Old Saybrook, CT: Globe Pequot Press, 1993.

PERIODICALS

Canoe & Kayak
P.O. Box 3146
Kirkland, WA 98083
(800) 692-2663
(206) 827-6363
Fax (206) 827-1893

Paddler
America Canoe Association (ACA)
7432 Alban Station Rd.
Suite B-226
Springfield, VA 22150
(703) 451-0141

Sea Kayaker
P.O. Box 17170
Seattle, WA 98107
(206) 789-9536

APPENDIX 2

KAYAK MANUFACTURERS

Ainsworth
P.O. Box 207
Norwich, VT 05055
(802) 649-2952
Fax (902) 649-2254

Aquaterra
(See Perception Inc.)

Baldwin Boat Co.
RR 2, Box 268
Orrington, ME 04474
(207) 825-4439

Baltic Kayaks
330 McKinley Terrace
Centerport, NY 11721
(516) 673-4662
Fax (516) 673-8352

Betsie Bay Kayak
P.O. Box 1706
Frankfort, MI 49635
(616) 352-7774

Boreal Design
108 Amsterdam
Industrial Park
St. Augustin, Quebec, G3A 1V9
Canada
(418) 878-3099
Fax (418) 878-3459

Cal-Tek Engineering
36 Riverside Dr.
Kingston, MA 02364
(617) 585-5666

Chesapeake Light Craft
1805 George Ave.
Annapolis, MD 21401
(410) 267-0137
Fax (301) 858-6335

Current Designs
10124 McDonald Pk. Rd.
Sidney, British Columbia V8L 5X8
Canada
(604) 655-1822
Fax (604) 655-1596

Dagger Canoe Co.
P.O. Box 1500
Harriman, TN 37748
(423) 882-0404
Fax (423) 882-8153

Easy Rider Canoe & Kayak Co.
P.O. Box 88108
Seattle, WA 98138
(425) 228-3633
Fax (425) 277-8778

Eddyline Kayaks
1344 Ashten Rd.
Burlington, WA 98233
(360) 757-2300

Englehart Products Inc. (EPI)
P.O. Box 377
Newbury, OH 44065
(216) 564-5565
Fax (216) 564-5515

Euro Kayaks/TG Canoe Livery
P.O. Box 177
Martindale, TX 78655
(512) 353-3946 or 3947

Glenwa, Inc.
P.O. Box 3134
Gardena, CA 90247
(310) 327-9216
Fax (310) 327-8952

Great Canadian Canoe Co.
64 Worcester Providence Tpke. (Rt. 146)
Sutton, MA 01590
(508) 865-0010
Fax (508) 865-5220

Hop on Top Kayaks
P.O. Box 139
Jamestown, RI 02835
(401) 423-1815
Fax (401) 423-1815

Hydra Kayaks
5061 S. National Dr.
Knoxville, TN 37914
(800) 537-8888
Fax (305) 836-1296

Impex International
(See P&H Designs and Pyranha)

Island Innovations Inc.
738 Selkirk Ave.
Victoria, British Columbia V9A 2T5
Canada
(250) 388-7466

Janautica/Splashdance
Hwy. 85 South
Niceville, FL 32578
(850) 678-1637
Fax (850) 678-1637

Jumbo/Pouch
1931 SW 14th St. #3
Portland, OR 97201
(503) 274-2313
Fax (503) 243-2159

Kayak Lab, Inc.
18 Regina Dr.
Chelmsford, MA 01824
(978) 256-5515
Fax (978) 256-5515

Kiwi Kayak Co.
2454 Vista Del Monte
Concord, CA 94520
(510) 692-2041
Fax (510) 692-2042

Kruger Canoes
2906 Meister Ln.
Lansing, MI 48906
(517) 323-2139

Mainstream Products, Inc.
182 Kayaker Way
Easley, SC 29642
(517) 323-2139

Mariner Kayaks, Inc.
2134 Westlake Ave. N.
Seattle, WA 98109
(206) 284-8404
Fax (206) 284-6046

Mega/Impex International
1107 Station Rd.
Bellport, NY 11713
(516) 286-1988
Fax (516) 286-1952

Necky Kayaks, Ltd.
1100 Riverside Rd.
Abbotsford, British Columbia V25 7P1
Canada
(604) 850-1206
Fax (604) 850-3197

Nigel Dennis Kayaks/Great River Outfitters
3721 Shallow Brook
Bloomfield Hills, MI 48302
(248) 644-6909
Fax (248) 644-4960

Nomad Kayaks
4918 Boul. Rive Sud
Levis, Quebec G6W 5N6
Canada
(418) 838-0338
Fax (418) 838-0801

Northwest Kayaks, Inc.
15145 NE 90th St.
Redmond, WA 98052
(425) 869-1107
Fax (425) 869-9014

Ocean Kayak, Inc.
P.O. Box 5003
Ferndale, WA 98248
(800) 852-9257
Fax (360) 366-2628

Old Town Canoe Co.
58 Middle St.
Old Town, ME 04468
(207) 827-5513
Fax (207) 827-2779

P&H Designs/Impex International
1107 Station Rd., Unit 1
Bellport, NY 11713
(516) 286-1988
Fax (516) 286-1952

Pacific Water Sports Inc.
16055 Pacific Hwy. S.
Seattle, WA 98188
(206) 246-9358
Fax (206) 439-9040

Perception Inc.
P.O. Box 8002
Easley, SC 29641
(803) 859-7518
Fax (803) 855-5995

Phoenix Poke Boats, Inc.
P.O. Box 109
207 N. Broadway
Berea, KY 40403-0109
(606) 986-2336
Fax (606) 986-3277

Prijon/Wildwasser Sport USA
P.O. Box 4617
Boulder, CO 80306
(303) 444-2336
Fax (303) 444-2375

Pygmy Boats Inc.
P.O. Box 1529
Pt. Townsend, WA 98368
(360) 385-6143
Fax (360) 379-9326

Pyranha/Impex International
1107 Station Rd.
Bellport, NY 11713
(516) 286-1988
Fax (516) 286-1952

Rainforest Designs Ltd.
P.O. Box 91
Maple Ridge, British Columbia V0M 1B0
Canada
(604) 467-9932
Fax (604) 467-8890

Seaward Kayaks Ltd.
RR 1, Site 16
Summerland, British Columbia V0H 1Z0
Canada
(800) 595-9755
Fax (250) 494-5200

Seda Products
926 Coolidge Ave.
National City, CA 91950
(619) 336-2444
Fax (619) 336-2405

Southern Exposure Sea Kayaks
P.O. Box 4530
Tequesta, FL 33469
(561) 575-4530
Fax (561) 744-9371

Superior Kayaks
P.O. Box 355
Whitelaw, WI 54247
(414) 732-3784

Swift Canoe & Kayak
RR #1 Oxtongue Lake
Dwight, Ontario P0A 1H0
Canada
(705) 635-1167

Trent Canoe & Kayak
2350 Haines Rd.
Bldg. 28
Mississauga, Ontario L4Y 1Y6
Canada
(905) 273-9075
Fax (905) 275-3090

Tsunami
13732 Bear Mountain Rd.
Redding, CA 96003
(916) 275-4313
Fax (916) 275-3090

The Upstream Edge (Rockwood Outfitters)
699 Speedvale Ave. W.
Guelph, Ontario N1K 1E6
Canada
(519) 824-1415
Fax (519) 824-8750

Valhalla Surf Ski Products
4724 Renex Pl.
San Diego, CA 92117
(619) 569-1395
Fax (619) 569-0295

Valley Canoe Products/Great River Outfitters
3721 Shallow Brook
Bloomfield Hills, MI 48302
(248) 644-6909
Fax (248) 644-4960

Vermont Canoe Products
R.R. 1, Box 353A
Newport, VT 05855
(800) 454-2307
Fax (802) 754-2307

Walden Paddlers, Inc.
152 Commonwealth Ave.
Concord, MA 01742
(508) 371-3000

West Side Boat Shop
7661 Tanawanda Creek Rd.
Lockport, NY 14094
(716) 434-5755

Wet Willy Kayaks
6978 Hollywood St.
Coos Bay, OR 97420
(541) 888-8173

Wilderness Systems
P.O. Box 4339
Archdale, NC 27263
(910) 434-7470
Fax (910) 434-6912

Woodstrip Watercraft Co.
1818 Swamp Pike
Gilbertsville, PA 19525
(610) 326-9282

APPENDIX 3

SOURCES OF ACCESSORIES

Cascade Outfitters
P.O. Box 209
Springfield, OR 97477
(800) 223-7238
(503) 747-2272

Colorado Kayak Supply
P.O. Box 3059
Buena Vista, CO 81211
(800) 535-3565
(719) 395-2422
Fax (719) 395-2421

Four Corners River Sports
P.O. Box 379
Durango, CO 81302
(800) 426-7637
(970) 259-3893
Fax (970) 247-7819

Great River Outfitters
3721 Shallow Brook
Bloomfield Hills, MI 48302
(810) 683-4770

Jersey Paddler
Route 88W
Brick, NJ 08724
(908) 458-5777

Nantahala Outdoor Center Outfitter Store
13077 Hwy. 19 West
Bryson City, NC 28713
(800) 367-7521

NOC Outfitter's Store
13077 Hwy. 19 West
Byson City, NC 28713
(800) 367-3521
(704) 488-6737
Fax (704) 488-8039

Northwest River Supplies
2009 South Maine
Moscow, ID 83843
(800) 635-5202
(208) 882-2383
Fax (208) 883-4787

Piragis Northwoods Company
105 North Central Ave.
Ely, MN 55731
(800) 223-6565

Recreational Equipment, Inc.
1700 45th St. East
Sumner, WA 98390
(800) 426-4840

Thule
42 Silverman Rd.
Seymour, CT 06843
(800) 238-2388

Wildwater Designs
230 Penllyn Pike
Penllyn, PA 19422
(215) 646-5034

Wyoming River Raiders
601 Wyoming Blvd.
Casper, WY 82609
(800) 247-6068
(307) 235-8624

Yakima Products
P.O. Box 4899
Arcata, CA 95518
(707) 826-8000

GLOSSARY

asymmetrical. Hull shape in which the kayak's widest point is either ahead of or behind its center

beam. Width of a kayak measured at the widest point

bilge. Transitional area where the hull's bottom turns up into its sides; see also **chine**

boulder garden. A rapid densely strewn with boulders

bow. Front of the boat

brace. Technique used to stabilize a tipping kayak; the low brace and high brace are two common techniques

breaking wave. A standing wave that falls upstream

broach. Occurs when a kayak becomes caught in the current against an obstruction and is turned sideways; considered very dangerous and often results in severe damage as the current's force wraps the boat around the obstruction; also occurs when current differentials at the bow and stern force a kayak into an abrupt sideways turn

broaching sea. Waves and swell coming at the side of the boat, usually making handling more difficult than with other boat angles to the wind; also called beam sea

bulkhead. Sealed compartment required primarily for flotation but also used as storage area with access via deck hatches

chine. Edge of the kayak; the transition area between hull and deck; see also **bilge**

coaming. Curved lip around the edge of the cockpit, used to secure the spray skirt

cockpit. Opening in the deck of a kayak where the paddler sits; "keyhole" cockpits are elongated to allow easier and safer entry and emergency exits, especially in whitewater.

cubic feet per second. (cfs) a measurement of the volume of water flowing past a given point per second

dead reckoning. Method of calculating distance from time on the water and estimated paddling speed

deck. Closed-in area over the bow and stern of a kayak that sheds water

depth. Vertical measurement from the hull's lowest point to its highest

directional stability. Tendency of a kayak to hold its course when under way; see also **tracking**

draw stroke. Used to move the boat sideways; performed by placing the paddle into the water parallel to the boat at an arm's reach away, then pulling the boat over to it

drop. Steep, sudden vertical change in a riverbed

eddy. Area in the river where the current either stops or moves upstream—opposite the main current—usually found below obstructions and on the inside of bends

eddy line. Transitional area between the main current and the eddy current; see also **eddy**

entrapment. Often dangerous situation in which a boat or paddler is held fast by the current or an obstacle; see also **broach, pin**

Eskimo roll. Self-rescue technique used to right an overturned kayak in the water without leaving the boat

feather. To turn the blade of a paddle horizontal to the water

ferry. Maneuver used to cross a current with little or no downstream travel that uses the current's force to move the boat laterally

fiberglass. Glass-fiber cloth impregnated with resin that can be easily formed into hull shapes; relatively cheap, durable, and easy to repair

final stability. Describes a boat's resistance to tipping once the boat has been leaned to a point beyond its initial stability; also called secondary stability

flare. Describes a hull cross section that grows increasingly wider as it rises from the water line toward the gunwales

flatwater. Lake water or slow-moving river current with no rapids

flotation bags. Inflatable buoyancy bags added to a kayak to ensure that it does not sink when swamped

following sea. Waves and swell coming from the stern of a boat

grab loop. Short rope or grab-handle threaded through the bow and stern of a kayak, most often used as a carrying handle, but also good for catching swimmers

hatch. Access port on front or rear deck of a touring or sea kayak

hull. Bottom of a kayak

hull configuration. Shape of the hull or that part affected by water, wind, and waves

hypothermia. Serious medical condition caused by lowering of body temperature, requiring immediate first aid

initial stability. Describes a boat's resistance to leaning or its "tippiness"; see also **secondary stability**

keel. Strip or extrusion along the bottom of a boat to prevent side slipping; also adds rigidity or structural support to the boat

keel line. Longitudinal shape of the kayak's bottom; see also **hull configuration**

Kevlar. Fiber used as a material for kayak construction that is considerably lighter in weight (30 to 40 percent), has greater resistance, and is higher priced than fiberglass

lay-up. Manner in which layers of fiberglass or Kevlar are assembled to make a kayak

pin. Situation in which a boat is caught broadside on an obstruction, most common on steep, shallow rivers; see also **broach, entrapment**

polyethylene. Thermoplastic material used in the construction of kayaks

portaging. Traditional term for carrying boats and gear, usually around rapids or between lakes

pry stroke. Turning stroke in which the paddle blade is turned sideways alongside the boat, then pushed outward

rocker. Upward curvature of the keel line from the center toward the ends of a kayak; see also **hull configuration, keel line, tracking**

rudder. Steering device on touring or sea kayaks

secondary stability. Hull's tendency to stabilize as it's leaned to one side; see also **hull configuration, initial stability**

shuttle. Process of leaving a vehicle at the trip's take-out to return boaters to vehicles left at the put-in

skeg. Fixed rudder

spray skirt. Neoprene or nylon "skirt" worn by kayakers to seal the cockpit

standing wave. High wave caused by slowing of the current

stern. Back end of a boat

strainer. Obstruction in the water that allows the current to pass through but stops any object floating or submerged

sweep stroke. Used to turn the boat by reaching out and ahead, then making a stroke in a wide arc

sweeper. Fallen trees or brush lying in the path of the current

symmetrical. Hull shape in which the kayak's widest point is at its center; see also **asymmetrical**

tandem. Two-person kayak

tracking. Ability of a boat to hold a straight course due to its design; see also **directional stability**

trim. Describes a boat that is level, side-to-side and end-to-end; achieved by shifting the load or position of the paddlers

tumblehome. Hull that curves inward from the water line toward the gunwales; see also **water line**

volume. Overall internal capacity of a kayak

water line. Position of water along the hull of a boat